# GCSE Music
## The Revision Guide

- Also perfect for grade exams

- Clear and concise

- 99.8% Spice Girl free

Published by Coordination Group Publications Ltd.

Main Author:
Elena Delaney
Further Contributors:
Catherine Baird, Martin Chester, Taissa Csaky, Chris Dennett, Dominic Hall, Rob Hall,
Peter Maries, Rebecca May, Katherine Reed, Glenn Rogers, Julie Schofield, Rachel Selway,
Alice Shwepperson (provided soft drinks throughout the project), Claire Thompson.


With thanks to John Furniss and Maria Lynch for the proofreading.

ISBN: 1-84146-789-8
Groovy website: www.cgpbooks.co.uk

Jolly bits of clipart from CorelDRAW

Printed by Elanders Hindson, Newcastle upon Tyne

# Contents

# SECTION ONE — THE BASICS

You might _know_ the stuff on this page already. Then again you might _think_ you know it all but be wrong about a couple of things. Or you might think you don't know _anything_ when in fact you know _everything_. There's _only one way_ to find out. Read it all and _learn it_ before you read on.

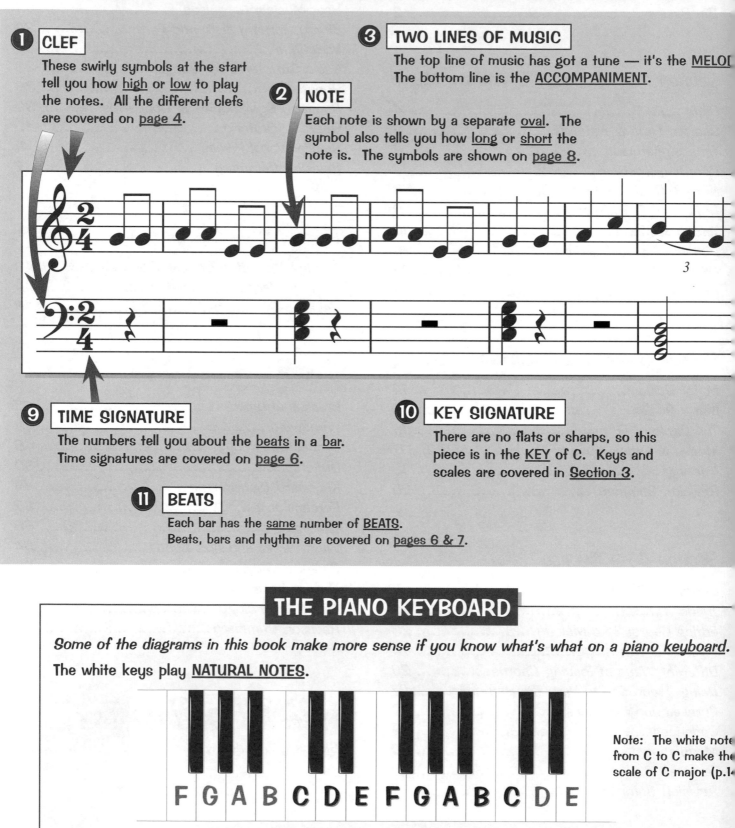

**① CLEF**

These swirly symbols at the start tell you how _high_ or _low_ to play the notes. All the different clefs are covered on _page 4_.

**② NOTE**

Each note is shown by a separate _oval_. The symbol also tells you how _long_ or _short_ the note is. The symbols are shown on _page 8_.

**③ TWO LINES OF MUSIC**

The top line of music has got a tune — it's the _MELO[_
The bottom line is the _ACCOMPANIMENT_.

**⑨ TIME SIGNATURE**

The numbers tell you about the _beats_ in a _bar_. Time signatures are covered on _page 6_.

**⑩ KEY SIGNATURE**

There are no flats or sharps, so this piece is in the _KEY_ of C. Keys and scales are covered in _Section 3_.

**⑪ BEATS**

Each bar has the _same_ number of _BEATS_. Beats, bars and rhythm are covered on _pages 6 & 7_.

## THE PIANO KEYBOARD

Some of the diagrams in this book make more sense if you know what's what on a _piano keyboard_. The white keys play _NATURAL NOTES_.

Note: The white note[
from C to C make the
scale of C major (p.1[

The black keys play _SHARPS_ and _FLATS_. Sharps and flats are covered on _page 5_.

The C right in the centre of a piano keyboard is known as _MIDDLE C_.

**⑤ LEMON**
A shiny yellow <u>fruit</u>.

**⑥ ELVIS**
Uh-huh.

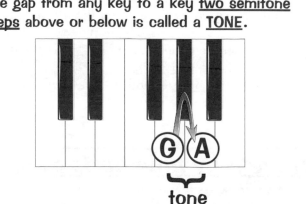

**BAR**
The vertical bar lines split the music into <u>bars</u>.

bar line

**⑦ STAVE**
The five lines are called a <u>stave</u>. Notes can go <u>on</u> or <u>between</u> the lines, or on separate short lines above or below.

**⑧ TRIPLETS**
The three along with the curved line shows these notes are <u>triplets</u>. They're explained on <u>page 9</u>.

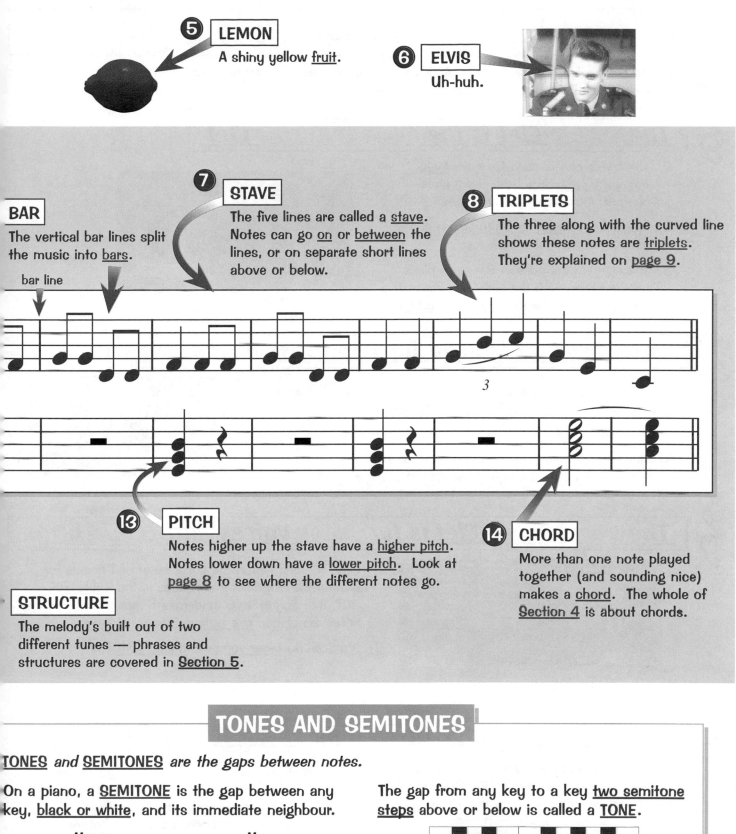

*3*

**⑬ PITCH**
Notes higher up the stave have a <u>higher pitch</u>. Notes lower down have a <u>lower pitch</u>. Look at <u>page 8</u> to see where the different notes go.

**⑭ CHORD**
More than one note played together (and sounding nice) makes a <u>chord</u>. The whole of <u>Section 4</u> is about chords.

**STRUCTURE**
The melody's built out of two different tunes — phrases and structures are covered in <u>Section 5</u>.

## TONES AND SEMITONES

<u>TONES</u> and <u>SEMITONES</u> are the gaps between notes.

On a piano, a <u>SEMITONE</u> is the gap between any key, <u>black or white</u>, and its immediate neighbour.

The gap from any key to a key <u>two semitone steps</u> above or below is called a <u>TONE</u>.

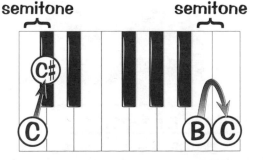

semitone          semitone

C#

C                    B  C

G  A

tone

# Clefs

Clefs are the <u>squiggly symbols</u> that you find right at the <u>start</u> of most written music.
The treble clef's used for high-pitched music. The bass and alto clefs are used for lower-pitched music.

## The Treble Clef is the Most Common Clef

1) The treble clef is used for quite <u>high</u>, <u>melody instruments</u>, e.g. flute, oboe, clarinet, violin, trumpet and horn.

2) Music for <u>soprano</u> and <u>alto</u> voices is written on the treble clef, too.

3) The sign always goes in the same place on the stave, with the curly bit wrapped around the line for the <u>G above middle C</u>.

MIDDLE C

## The Bass Clef is used for Low, Bass Instruments

1) The bass clef is used for <u>low</u>, <u>bass instruments</u> like the tuba, trombone, bassoon, cello and double bass.

2) It's also used for <u>bass voices</u>.

3) The big blob always goes on the line for the <u>F below middle C</u>, and the two little dots go either side of the line.

MIDDLE C

## The Vocal Tenor Clef is for Tenor Voices and Lead Guitar

1) Each line and gap in the vocal tenor clef stands for exactly the same note as it does in the <u>treble clef</u>, BUT, that tiny little '<u>8</u>' underneath means that the notes are played <u>one octave</u> (see p.18) <u>lower</u>.

2) It's used by <u>tenor voices</u> and <u>lead guitar</u> parts.

HERE IT IS.    MIDDLE C

## The C Clef can Move Up and Down on the Stave

The C clef always has its <u>middle point</u> on <u>middle C</u>. It can be used as 2 different clefs, depending on its <u>position</u> on the stave.

1) When its middle point is on the <u>middle line</u>, it's the <u>alto clef</u> and is used for <u>viola</u> parts.

MIDDLE C

2) When the middle point is on the <u>fourth line up</u>, it's called the <u>tenor clef</u>, which is used for the <u>higher notes</u> in <u>bass instruments</u> like trombones, bassoons and double basses.

MIDDLE C

## There'll be blue birds over... the white clefs of Dover...

I know, I know — the vocal tenor and C clefs are about as common as giant pandas, but you've got to know what they are when you <u>do</u> see them. Aim to get so good at reading and writing on the <u>treble</u> and <u>bass</u> clefs that you can do it in a plague of thunderflies. They're written out in full on <u>page 8</u>.

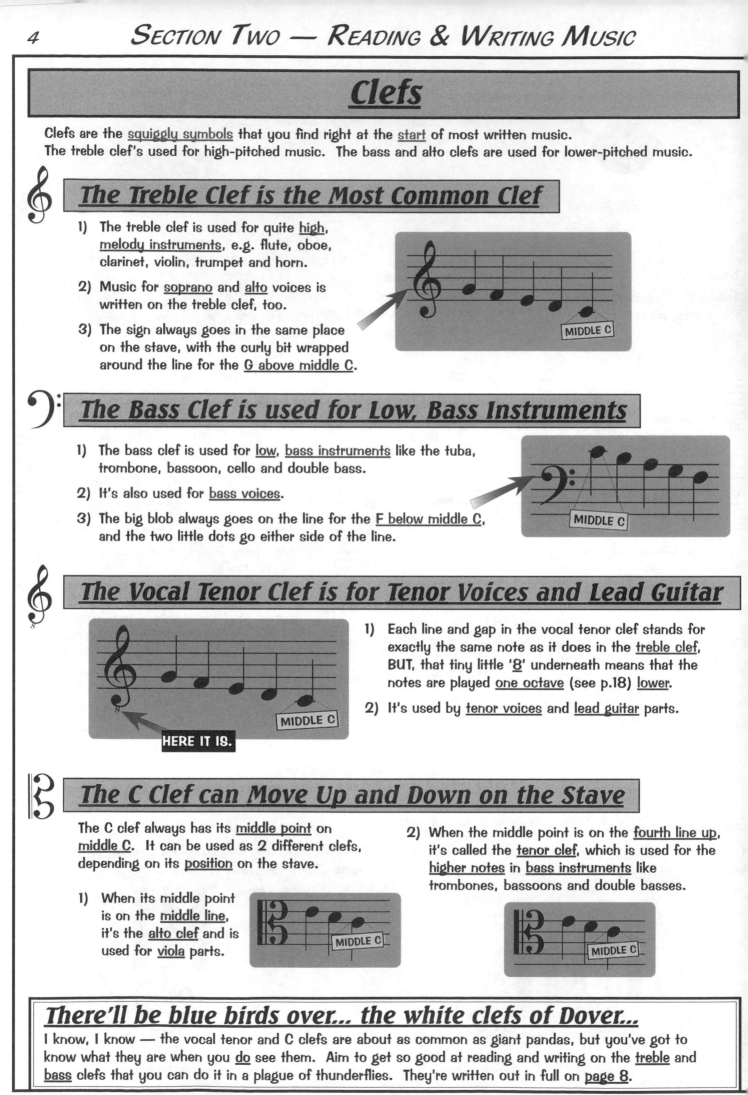

# Sharps, Flats & Naturals

On a piano, <u>natural</u> notes are the <u>white</u> ones. <u>Sharps</u> are the <u>black</u> notes to the <u>right</u> of the white notes. <u>Flats</u> are the notes to the <u>left</u> of the white notes. So each black note is both sharp <u>and</u> flat. Clever stuff.

## ♯ A Sharp Makes a Note Slightly Higher

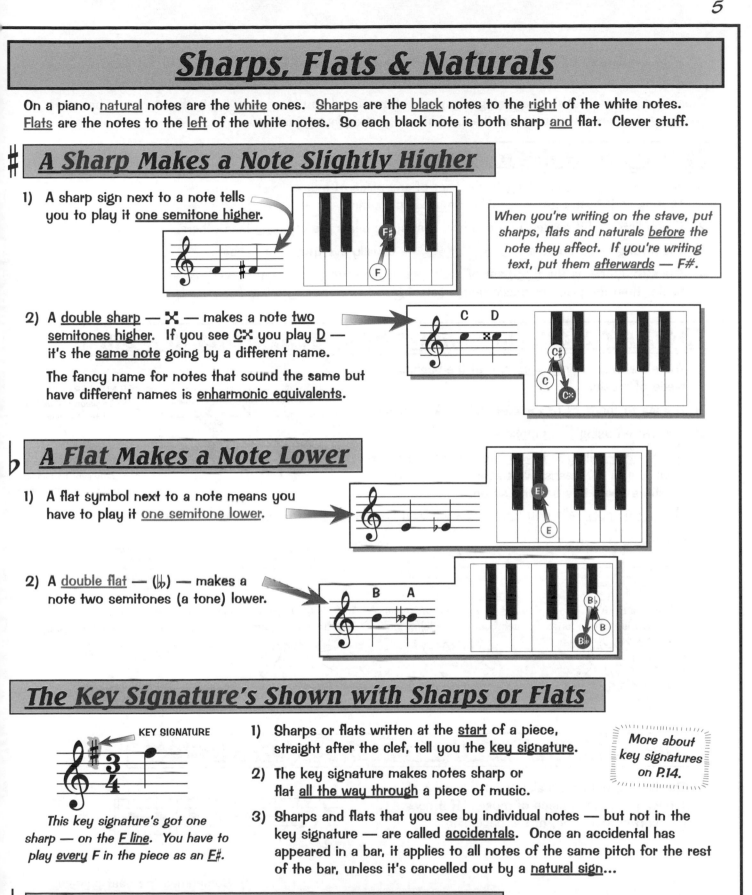

1) A sharp sign next to a note tells you to play it <u>one semitone higher</u>.

> When you're writing on the stave, put sharps, flats and naturals <u>before</u> the note they affect. If you're writing text, put them <u>afterwards</u> — F♯.

2) A <u>double sharp</u> — 𝄪 — makes a note <u>two semitones higher</u>. If you see C𝄪 you play <u>D</u> — it's the <u>same note</u> going by a different name.

The fancy name for notes that sound the same but have different names is <u>enharmonic equivalents</u>.

C   D

## ♭ A Flat Makes a Note Lower

1) A flat symbol next to a note means you have to play it <u>one semitone lower</u>.

2) A <u>double flat</u> — (𝄫) — makes a note two semitones (a tone) lower.

B   A

## The Key Signature's Shown with Sharps or Flats

KEY SIGNATURE

This key signature's got one sharp — on the <u>F line</u>. You have to play <u>every</u> F in the piece as an <u>F♯</u>.

1) Sharps or flats written at the <u>start</u> of a piece, straight after the clef, tell you the <u>key signature</u>.

2) The key signature makes notes sharp or flat <u>all the way through</u> a piece of music.

3) Sharps and flats that you see by individual notes — but not in the key signature — are called <u>accidentals</u>. Once an accidental has appeared in a bar, it applies to all notes of the same pitch for the rest of the bar, unless it's cancelled out by a <u>natural sign</u>...

More about key signatures on P.14.

## A Natural Sign Cancels a Sharp or Flat

A <u>natural</u> sign before a note <u>cancels</u> the <u>effect of a sharp or flat</u> sign from earlier in the bar or from a key signature.

You <u>never</u> see natural signs in the key signature, only in the music, as accidentals.

## This stuff should all come naturally in no time...

Double sharps and flats are very <u>rare</u> and quite weird — it doesn't seem that <u>logical</u> to write C𝄪 when you could write D. It all depends what key you're in. Weird, but then that's music for you.

# Time Signatures

Those <u>two numbers</u> at the beginning of a piece of music tell you <u>how many beats</u> there are in a bar and <u>how long</u> they are. If you ignore them, whatever you're playing just sounds like a <u>gloopy mess</u>.

## Music Has a Regular Beat

1) You can tap your foot along to the <u>beat</u> of any piece of music, so long as it hasn't got a horribly complicated rhythm.

2) If you listen a bit harder, you can hear that some beats are <u>stronger</u> than others.

3) The strong beats come at <u>regular intervals</u> — usually every <u>2</u>, <u>3</u> or <u>4</u> beats.

4) The strong beat is the <u>first</u> beat of each <u>bar</u>. If the strong beat comes every 3 beats, then the piece of music you're listening to has <u>three beats</u> in a bar.

## The Time Signature Shows How Many Beats in a Bar

1) There's always a <u>time signature</u> at the beginning of a piece of music.

2) It goes to the <u>right</u> of the clef and the key signature.

3) It's written using <u>two numbers</u>.

TOP NUMBER
goes between the middle line and the top line

The <u>top number</u> tells you <u>how many beats</u> there are in each bar, e.g. a '2' means two beats in a bar, a '3' means three beats in a bar and so on.

BOTTOM NUMBER
goes between the middle line and the bottom line

The <u>bottom number</u> tells you <u>how long</u> each beat is (see <u>page 8</u> for names of different notes).

A <u>2</u> at the bottom means each beat is <u>1 minim</u> long.
**2 = ♩**

A <u>4</u> at the bottom means each beat is <u>1 crotchet</u> long.
**4 = ♩**

An <u>8</u> at the bottom means each beat is <u>1 quaver</u> long.
**8 = ♪**

A <u>16</u> at the bottom means each beat is <u>1 semiquaver</u> long.
**16 = ♪**

## If the Beat Changes the Time Signature Changes

1) The time signature usually <u>stays the same</u> all the way through a piece of music. If it does, it's written just <u>once</u>, at the beginning.

1  2  1  2  1  2

1  2  1  2  1  2    1  2  3  1  2  3

2) Sometimes the beat <u>changes</u> during a piece. If it does, the new time signature's written in the bar where it <u>changes</u>.

## Music's just like 50s New York — beats everywhere... *

* This is a very <u>pretentious</u> comment, referring to the "Beat Generation" of writers who were around in New York in 1950s. It's so pretentious that I wouldn't be surprised if you <u>ripped this book up</u> in annoyance. But then how would you get through your Music GCSE...

# Counting the Beat

Counting the beat's fairly easy, but it's a pretty crucial skill. It'll help you work out how to play a piece you don't know and how to write a tune down when you've only heard it on a CD or in your head.

## In Simple Time You Count All the Beats

1) Simple time signatures have 2, 3, or 4 as their top number.

2) In simple time, if you're counting to the music, you count every beat.
For $\frac{4}{4}$ you'd count "One, two, three, four." For $\frac{3}{2}$, you'd count "One, two, three."

3) If you want to count out the rhythm of smaller notes as well as the beats, try using "and", "eye" and "a" — it seems to make the rhythm come out just right.

> Count "One and two and" for quavers, and "One eye and a" for semiquavers.
> $\frac{2}{4}$ 1 2 | 1 and 2 and | 1 eye and a 2 eye and a

4) Any shorter notes are usually a half, a quarter, an eighth or a sixteenth of the main beat.

## In Compound Time Only Count the Big Beats

1) Compound time signatures have 6, 9 or 12 as their top number — you can always divide the top number by three.

2) It's too awkward to count to nine or twelve for every bar. You end up with so many little beats that the rhythm sounds mushy.

3) To make the rhythm clear, every set of three beats is grouped into one:
$\frac{6}{8}$ 1 2

4) If you were counting out the main beats in $\frac{6}{8}$, you'd count, "One, two. One, two." $\frac{9}{8}$ would go "One, two, three. One, two, three."
$\frac{9}{8}$ 1 2 3 1 & a 2 & a 3 & a

5) To count the in-between notes, use "and" and "a".

6) Shorter notes are made by dividing by three — so they're thirds, sixths, twelfths etc. of the main beat.

7) Music in compound time sounds different from music in simple time — practise spotting the difference.

## The Patterns the Beats Make are Called the Metre

Depending on the time signature, the beats make different patterns.
The pattern is known as the metre. Metre can be:

**REGULAR**
The strong beats make the same pattern all the way through.
TWO beats per bar = duple metre
THREE beats per bar = triple metre
FOUR beats per bar = quadruple metre

**IRREGULAR**
There could be five or seven beats in a bar grouped in twos, threes and fours within each bar.

**FREE**
Music with no particular metre. This one's fairly unusual.

Zzzzzzzzzzzzzzzzzzzzzzzzzzzzzzzzzzzzzzzzzzzzzzzzzzzzzzzzzzzzzz...
What?! Oh, sorry. Thought you said counting sheep. Anyway, counting the beat's not really that hard. The tricky bit on this page is the stuff about metre. You could get asked what kind of metre something's in in your listening exam so learn all three sorts. And give me back my duvet.

# Note & Rest Symbols

Let's face it, you'd be a bit lost reading music if you didn't know what all those funny little dots and squiggles meant. Make sure you know all this stuff <u>better than the alphabet</u>.

## The Symbols Tell You How Long Notes and Rests Are

1) <u>Note</u> symbols tell you how many beats to hold a <u>sound</u> for.

2) <u>Rest</u> symbols tell you how many beats to hold a <u>silence</u> for.

3) Notes and rests have <u>names</u>, depending on how long they are.
   Two beats is a <u>minim</u> note or rest. A half-beat is a <u>quaver</u> note or rest.

Learn this table now — you need to know exactly how to <u>write</u> these out, and how to <u>play</u> them.

| NAME OF NOTE | NUMBER OF CROTCHET BEATS | NOTE SYMBOL | REST SYMBOL |
|---|---|---|---|
| **semibreve** <br> whole note * | 4 | o | ▬ |
| **minim** <br> half note * | 2 | ♩ | ▬ |
| **crotchet** <br> quarter note * | 1 | ♩ | 𝄽 |
| **quaver** <br> eighth note * | ½ | ♪ or ♫ <br> ...if there's 2 or more. | 𝄾 |
| **semiquaver** <br> sixteenth note * | ¼ | ♬ or ♬ <br> ...if there's 2 or more. | 𝄿 |

I'm terribly sorry, I have absolutely no idea what you're talking about.

Not everyone can read music.

*These are the <u>American</u> names for <u>note values</u>. Handy when your band's over there promoting your first album.*

## The Position of the Note Tells You the Pitch

<u>Just in case</u> you don't know one clef from another, this is where the notes go in the <u>bass</u> and <u>treble</u> clefs.

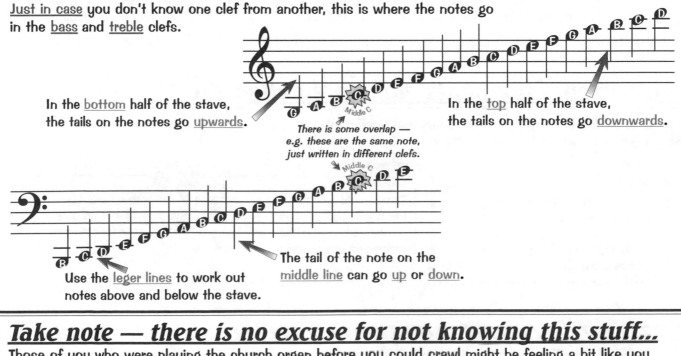

In the <u>bottom</u> half of the stave, the tails on the notes go <u>upwards</u>.

*There is some overlap — e.g. these are the same note, just written in different clefs.*

In the <u>top</u> half of the stave, the tails on the notes go <u>downwards</u>.

Use the <u>leger lines</u> to work out notes above and below the stave.

The tail of the note on the <u>middle line</u> can go <u>up</u> or <u>down</u>.

## Take note — there is no excuse for not knowing this stuff...

Those of you who were playing the church organ before you could <u>crawl</u> might be feeling a bit like you know this stuff already and you don't need to be told. Well, just check you do know it. Pride comes before a fall, as the revision guide writer said to the...*AAAAGH!*

# Dots, Ties & Triplets

You can only get so far with the note lengths from page 8. If you use dot, tie and triplet symbols you can get more complicated, interesting and sophisticated rhythms. Leading to much wackiness and mirth.

## A Dot After a Note or Rest Makes it Longer

1) A dot just to the right of a note or rest makes it half as long again.

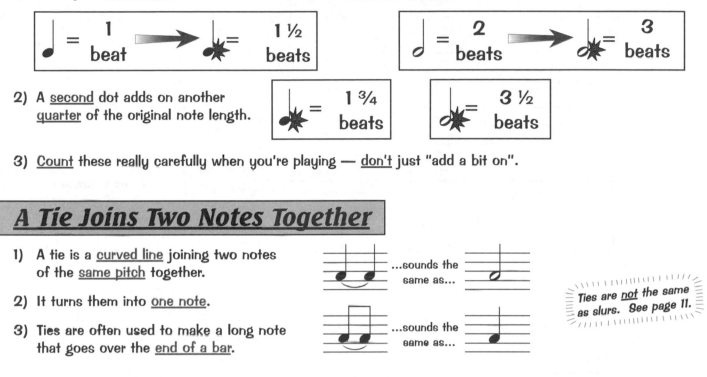

| ♩ = 1 beat | → | ✹ = 1 ½ beats | | 𝅗𝅥 = 2 beats | → | ✹ = 3 beats |

2) A second dot adds on another quarter of the original note length.

| ✹ = 1 ¾ beats | | ✹ = 3 ½ beats |

3) Count these really carefully when you're playing — don't just "add a bit on".

## A Tie Joins Two Notes Together

1) A tie is a curved line joining two notes of the same pitch together.

2) It turns them into one note.

3) Ties are often used to make a long note that goes over the end of a bar.

...sounds the same as...

...sounds the same as...

*Ties are not the same as slurs. See page 11.*

## A Triplet is Three Notes Played in the Time of Two

1) A triplet is three notes, all the same length, squeezed into the time of two.

2) Triplets are marked with a '3' above or below the middle of the three notes.

3) Sometimes there's a square bracket or a curved line as well as the three.

4) The notes don't all have to be played — part of a triplet can be rests.

---

## A piglet is one small pig in the space of one small pig...

Triplets. Grrrr. Bane of my life (well, one of them anyway). They look so straightforward on the page, then I try playing them and my fingers get tangled up, my head starts spinning... The only way to get on top of playing them is with a metronome. Boring but true.

# Tempo & Mood

Composers are <u>control freaks</u>. They don't just tell you the notes — they tell you <u>how fast</u> to play them, and what the <u>atmosphere</u> of the piece should be too. <u>Get your own back</u> with your own compositions.

## The Tempo is the Speed of the Main Beats

Tempo is Italian for "<u>time</u>". In a lot of music the instructions for how fast to play are written in Italian too. Here are the words you're <u>most</u> likely to come across:

| Italian Word | ...what it means... | Beats per Minute |
|---|---|---|
| largo | broad and slow | 40 - 60 |
| larghetto | still broad, not so slow | 60 - 66 |
| adagio | bit faster than largo | 66 - 76 |
| andante | walking pace | 76 - 108 |
| moderato | moderate speed | 108 - 120 |
| allegro | quick and lively | 120 - 168 |
| vivace | very lively — quicker than allegro | 168 - 180 |
| presto | really fast | 180 - 200 |

This is where you put the <u>tempo</u> and <u>beats per minute</u> on the stave.

Moderato (♩ = 110)

<u>60</u> beats a minute means each crotchet lasts <u>one</u> second. <u>120</u> beats a minute means each crotchet lasts <u>half a second</u>. And so on...

This lot tell you how to <u>vary</u> the speed. The <u>words</u> go <u>underneath</u> the stave. The <u>pause</u> symbol goes <u>above</u>.

| Italian Word | Abbreviations | ...what it means... |
|---|---|---|
| accelerando | accel. | speeding up |
| rallentando | rall. | slowing down |
| ritenuto | rit. | holding back the pace |
| allargando | allarg. | slowing down, getting a bit louder |
| rubato | rub. | can be flexible with pace of music |
| 𝆩 | | pause — longer than a whole beat |
| a tempo | | back to the original pace |

## Mood Is the Overall Feel of a Piece

Just for kicks, <u>mood</u>'s usually described in Italian too.

| Italian Word | ...what it means... |
|---|---|
| agitato | agitated |
| alla marcia | in a march style |
| amoroso | loving |
| calmato | calm |
| dolce | soft and sweet |
| energico | energetic |

| Italian Word | ...what it means... |
|---|---|
| giocoso | playful, humorous |
| grandioso | grandly |
| pesante | heavy |
| risoluto | strong, confident, bold |
| sospirando | sighing |
| trionfale | triumphant |

To describe the <u>overall mood</u> put the word at the beginning of the piece.

To describe a <u>change of mood</u> write the word under the stave.

## WHAT DO YOU MEAN, I'M "IN A MOOD"?!?...

When you're learning the Italian words, start with all the ones that sound a bit like English — they're easy. Once you've learnt them, cross them off. You'll find you've got a much <u>shorter</u> list to learn. Crafty, eh...

# Dynamics & Articulation

More cunning little devices for ensnaring players into playing your music _exactly_ how you want it to sound.

## Dynamic Markings Tell You How Loud or Quietly to Play

Music that was all played at the _same volume_ would be pretty dull.
To get a _variety_ of different volumes you can use these symbols:

| Symbol | ...stands for... | ...what it means... |
|---|---|---|
| _pp_ | _pianissimo_ | very quiet |
| _p_ | _piano_ | quiet |
| _mp_ | _mezzo piano_ | fairly quiet |
| _mf_ | _mezzo forte_ | fairly loud |
| _f_ | _forte_ | loud |
| _ff_ | _fortissimo_ | very loud |
| < | _crescendo_ | getting louder |
| > | _diminuendo_ | getting quieter |

The markings go _underneath_ the stave.

_Astonishingly, all these words are Italian. Now there's a surprise..._

ROAR

## Articulation Tells You How Much to Separate Notes

In theory all the notes of a bar should add up to one _continuous_ sound — but actually there are _tiny gaps_ between them. If you _exaggerate_ the gaps you get a _staccato_ effect. If you smooth the gaps out, the notes sound _slurred_.

STACCATO — All the dotted notes are played slightly short.

SLUR — All the notes below or above the slur are played smoothly, with no breaks between.

If the articulation goes _all the way through_ a piece, there's an overall instruction at the _beginning_.
(If it was to be played smoothly, the instruction would be "_legato_" here.)

Staccato

## Nothing to do with articulated lorries then...

Don't just learn the symbols. Learn what they're _called_ too — it'll sound way, way more impressive if you write about the "dynamics" in your listening exam than if you talk about the "loudness and quietness". Not that you'd do that of course. But I know people who would.

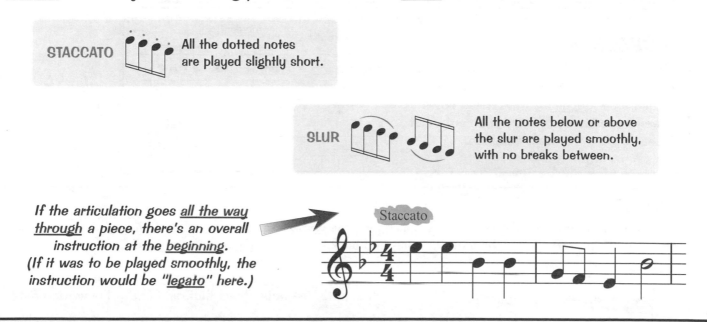

# Ornaments

Ornaments are fiddly <u>little notes</u> that stand out a bit from the main tune. There are <u>standard symbols</u> used to show all the main ornaments — but there's no standard way of playing them. It's up to the performer.

## A Trill is Lots of Tiny Quick Notes

1) If you see the symbol "<i>tr</i>", you play a <u>trill</u>.

2) If the music was written <u>before 1800</u>(ish) start one note <u>above</u> the written note then go quickly back and forth between the written note and the note you started on.

3) If the music was written <u>after 1800</u>(ish) <u>start on the written note</u> and trill up to the note above.

4) The <u>second last note</u> is usually the one <u>below</u> the written note.

5) A <u>sharp</u>, <u>flat</u> or <u>natural</u> sign above the trill symbol tells you if the note to trill to is sharp, flat or natural.

This is how you play the trill if the music's written after 1800.

The trill lasts the same length of time as the written note.

## Appoggiatura is an Extra Note in a Chord

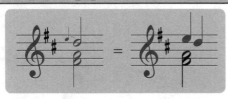

1) The appoggiatura starts on a note that <u>clashes</u> with the chord, then moves to a note that <u>belongs</u> in the chord.

2) The two notes are usually just <u>one tone</u> or <u>semitone</u> apart.

3) It normally takes <u>half the time value</u> of the note it 'leans' on.

More about appoggiaturas on <u>page 27</u>.

## Squeezing in a Tiny Note is Called Acciaccatura

"Acciaccatura" means <u>crushing in</u>. An acciaccatura in music is a note that's squeezed in before the main note and played <u>as fast as possible</u>.

## Mordents and Turns are Set Patterns of Notes

### MORDENTS

Mordents <u>start off</u> like trills. The difference is they <u>end</u> on the written note, which is played a bit <u>longer</u> than the trilled notes. There are loads of different mordents, but these two are the most common.

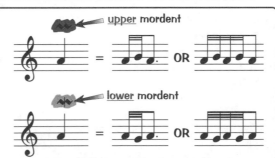

upper mordent

lower mordent

### TURNS

Start on the note <u>above</u> the written note, then play the <u>written note</u>, followed by the note <u>below</u> the written note. End back on the <u>written note</u>.

For an <u>inverted turn</u> play the note <u>below</u> the written note, the written note, the note above that, and finally the written note.

## China dogs, Spanish dancers, crystal swans and mordents...

The ornaments on this page are "standard" ones, mostly worked out in the <u>17th century</u>. They still get used nowadays. Jazz players use loads of ornaments, but they make their own up. That's jazz, baby...

# *Revision Summary*

You'll find a great wodge of questions like this at the end of every section. They're *NOT* here just to fill up space — they're here to <u>help you</u> test yourself. The basic idea is, if you can answer all the Revision Summary questions and stay as cool as a cucumber, you can be pretty darn sure you've understood and remembered all the important stuff. Look back through the section the first and second time you try the questions (if you must), but by the third time you do the questions, you should be aiming to get <u>all the answers right without looking</u>. I'm serious. Get on with it.

1) Does a clef tell you:
    a) how wide the stave is  b) what instrument it's for  or  c) how high or low the notes on it are?
2) Draw a stave with a treble clef at the beginning. Draw on middle C and mark on 16 letter names above middle C.
3) Draw a stave with a bass clef at the beginning. Draw on middle C and mark on 16 letter names below middle C.
4) Which voices read music from the treble clef?
5) Name two instruments that read music from the bass clef.
6) What's the difference between the symbol for a treble clef and the symbol for the vocal tenor clef?
7) Where does middle C go on a vocal tenor clef?
8) What <u>two</u> other names does the C clef go by?
9) Draw staves showing the C clef in both positions and write the correct name by each one.
10) Draw a sharp sign, a flat sign and a natural sign.
11) What does a sharp do to a note?
12) What does a flat do to a note?
13) Draw each of these signs and explain what you do if you see them by a note:
    a) a double sharp    b) a double flat
14) Draw a treble clef stave and add a key signature with an F sharp.
15) What do you call a sharp, flat or natural sign when it's in the music but not in the key signature?
16) One beat in the bar usually feels stronger than the others. Which one?
17) What do you call the two numbers at the start of a piece of music?
18) What does the top number tell you about the beats?
19) What does the bottom number tell you about the beats?
20) When a time signature changes in a piece of music, where's the new one written?
21) What's the difference between simple and compound time?
22) What's the difference between regular and irregular metre?
23) Draw the symbol for each of the following notes and write down how many crotchet beats it lasts:
    a) semibreve   b) minim   c) crotchet   d) quaver   e) semiquaver
24) What does a dot immediately after a note or rest do?
25) What's the time value of:
    a) a dotted crotchet    b) a dotted minim    c) a dotted semibreve    d) a double dotted minim?
26) What does a 'tie' do?
27) How much time, in crotchet beats, does a crotchet triplet take up?
28) Where do you put the tempo marking on a stave?
29) Which is slower, allegro or moderato?
30) Where would you write the word *agitato* on the stave?
31) How does a composer show on the written music that he wants the notes to be played smoothly?
32) What are the notes of an inverted turn starting on C?
33) What are the notes of an upper mordent starting on F?
34) Describe an appoggiatura.

*Section Two — Reading & Writing Music*

# Major Scales

There are two main types of scales — <u>major</u> and <u>minor</u>. Once you know how scales are put together, keys and chords make lots more sense. Honest.

## Ordinary Scales have Eight Notes

1) An ordinary major (or minor) scale has <u>8 notes</u>, starting and ending on notes of the <u>same name</u>, e.g. C major goes C, D, E, F, G, A, B, C.

*The gap between the bottom and top notes of a scale is called an <u>octave</u>. See P. 18.*

2) Each of the eight notes has a <u>name</u>.

| 1st note | 2nd note | 3rd note | 4th note | 5th note | 6th note | 7th note | 8th note |
|---|---|---|---|---|---|---|---|
| tonic | supertonic | mediant | subdominant | dominant | submediant | leading note | tonic |
| I | II | III | IV | V | VI | VII | VIII |

3) You can just use the <u>numbers</u> or the <u>Roman numerals</u> to name the notes too.

## Major Scales Sound Bright and Cheery

Whatever note they start on, all major scales sound <u>similar</u>, because they all follow the same <u>pattern</u>. The pattern's a set order of <u>tone</u> and <u>semitone</u> gaps between the notes:

I —tone→ II —tone→ III —semitone→ IV —tone→ V —tone→ VI —tone→ VII —semitone→ VIII

*Major scales <u>can</u> <u>start on any note</u>, including the black notes, e.g. C♯ major.*

This is how <u>C major</u> goes on a keyboard.

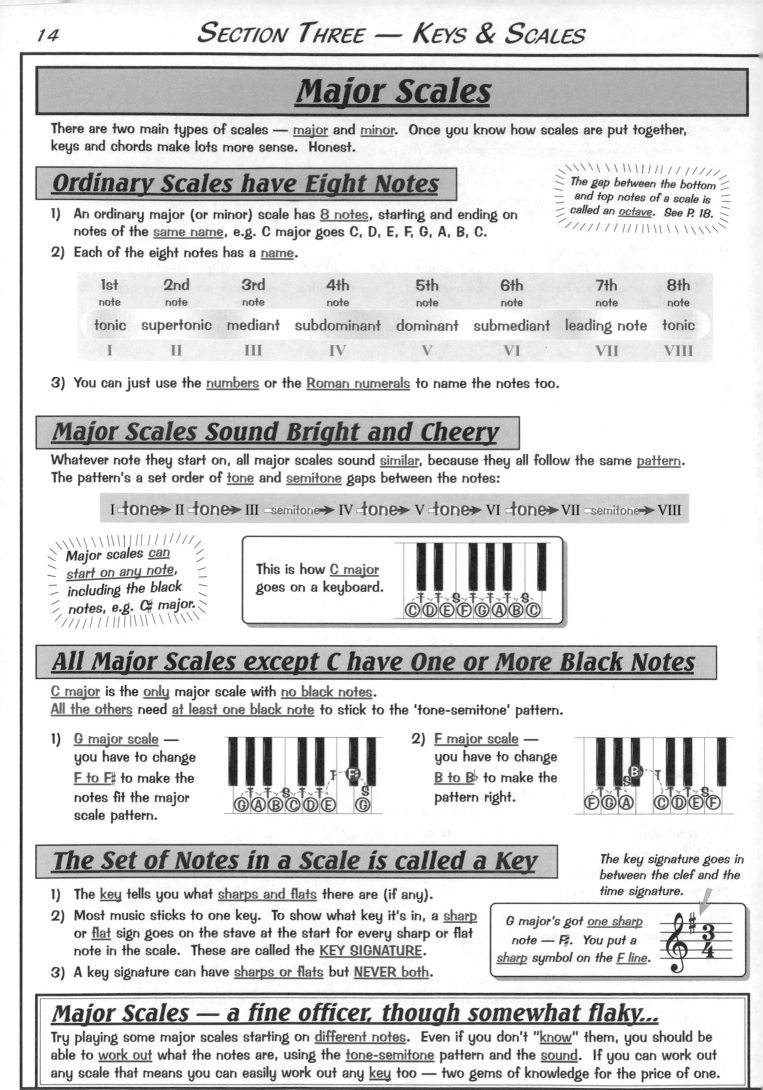

## All Major Scales except C have One or More Black Notes

<u>C major</u> is the <u>only</u> major scale with <u>no black notes</u>.
<u>All the others</u> need <u>at least one black note</u> to stick to the 'tone-semitone' pattern.

1) <u>G major scale</u> — you have to change <u>F to F♯</u> to make the notes fit the major scale pattern.

2) <u>F major scale</u> — you have to change <u>B to B♭</u> to make the pattern right.

## The Set of Notes in a Scale is called a Key

1) The <u>key</u> tells you what <u>sharps and flats</u> there are (if any).

2) Most music sticks to one key. To show what key it's in, a <u>sharp</u> or <u>flat</u> sign goes on the stave at the start for every sharp or flat note in the scale. These are called the <u>KEY SIGNATURE</u>.

3) A key signature can have <u>sharps or flats</u> but <u>NEVER both</u>.

*The key signature goes in between the clef and the time signature.*

G major's got <u>one sharp</u> note — F♯. You put a <u>sharp</u> symbol on the <u>F line</u>.

## Major Scales — a fine officer, though somewhat flaky...

Try playing some major scales starting on <u>different notes</u>. Even if you don't "<u>know</u>" them, you should be able to <u>work out</u> what the notes are, using the <u>tone-semitone</u> pattern and the <u>sound</u>. If you can work out any scale that means you can easily work out any <u>key</u> too — two gems of knowledge for the price of one.

# Minor Scales

Minor scales have fixed patterns too. Unfortunately, there are <u>three</u> different kinds you need to know.

## Minor Scales All Sound a Bit Mournful

Minor scales sound <u>completely different</u> from major scales, because they've got a different tone-semitone pattern. There are <u>three</u> types of minor scale, and all of them sound a bit <u>mournful</u>.

### 1) The Natural Minor Uses All the Same Notes as the Relative Major

These are easy. Start from the <u>sixth</u> note of any major scale. Carry on up to the same note an octave higher. You're playing a <u>natural minor scale</u>.

The sixth note of <u>C major</u> is <u>A</u>. If you play from <u>A to A</u> using the notes of C major, you're playing <u>A natural minor</u> (usually just called '<u>A minor</u>').

PAIRS OF KEYS LIKE <u>A MINOR AND C MAJOR</u> ARE CALLED "<u>RELATIVE</u>" KEYS.
A MINOR IS THE <u>RELATIVE MINOR</u> OF C MAJOR.
C MAJOR IS THE <u>RELATIVE MAJOR</u> OF A MINOR.

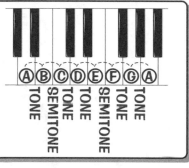

<u>All the notes</u> in a natural minor are <u>exactly the same</u> as the ones in the <u>relative major</u>. The <u>key signature</u>'s exactly the same too.

### 2) The Harmonic Minor has One Accidental

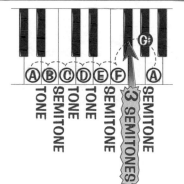

1) The <u>harmonic minor</u> has the same notes as the relative major, except for the <u>seventh note</u>.

2) The <u>seventh</u> note is always raised by <u>one semitone</u>.

3) You use the harmonic minor when you're writing <u>harmonies</u>. That <u>sharpened seventh note</u> makes the harmonies work much better than they would with notes from a natural minor. It's probably because it sort of feels like it wants to move up to the tonic.

### 3) The Melodic Minor has Two Accidentals to Make it More Tuneful

1) The <u>melodic minor</u> is just like a natural minor, using the notes from the relative major scale, <u>except for notes 6 and 7</u>.

2) On the way <u>up</u>, notes <u>6</u> and <u>7</u> are each <u>raised</u> by <u>one semitone</u>.

3) On the way <u>down</u>, the melodic minor goes just like the natural minor.

4) The melodic minor is used for writing <u>melodies</u>. Those two accidentals make tunes sound <u>smoother</u> by avoiding the big jump between notes 6 and 7 in the harmonic minor.

## And not forgetting the Morris Minor...

Three minor scales... couldn't they have stopped at two... You really do need to learn <u>all three</u> — names, notes, how they relate to the relative major, and what they're used for. All three have a gap of a <u>minor third</u> between the first and third notes in the scale — that's what makes them sound melancholy.

# The Circle of Fifths

The circle of fifths is a bit <u>mad-professorish</u>, but very <u>useful</u> — it tells you <u>all the keys</u>, all the <u>relative keys</u> and their <u>key signatures</u>.

## The Circle of Fifths Shows All the Keys

1) Altogether there are <u>12 major keys</u>. They're all shown on the <u>circle of fifths</u>.
2) Don't expect to fully get it if this is the first time you've seen it. Just <u>have a look</u> then read on.

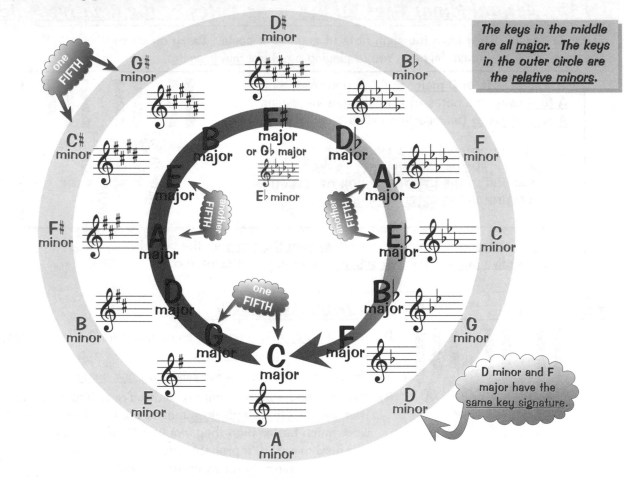

The keys in the middle are all <u>major</u>. The keys in the outer circle are the <u>relative minors</u>.

D minor and F major have the <u>same key signature</u>.

## Each Key Links to the Next One

1) The circle <u>starts</u> with <u>C major</u> at the bottom. The next key round is <u>G</u>. G's the <u>fifth note</u> of C major.
2) The fifth note of G major is D, the <u>next</u> key on the circle. This pattern repeats <u>all the way round</u>. That's why the chart's called the circle of fifths.
3) As you go round the circle the number of <u>sharps</u> in the <u>key signature</u> goes up <u>one</u> for each key.
4) When you get to <u>F♯ major</u> at the top there are <u>six sharps</u>. From here, you start writing the key signature in <u>flats</u> — you don't need as many so it's clearer to read.
5) The number of <u>flats</u> keeps going <u>down</u> until you get back to C major, with no sharps and no flats.

The <u>relative minors</u> in the outer circle work just the same way as the major keys — the <u>fifth note</u> of <u>A minor</u> is <u>E</u> and the next minor key's <u>E minor</u>... and so on. Don't forget you can always work out the relative minor by counting up to the <u>sixth note</u> of a major scale, (see P.15.) or the relative major by counting up to the <u>third note</u> of the minor scale.

## This is making my head spin...

In one way the circle of fifths is very <u>simple</u>. Then if you think about it too much it turns into a total <u>mind-frier</u>. Memorise it if you want, but you're better off remembering how it works, then you can always <u>work out</u> what you need to know.

# Modes & Other Types of Scales

Most music uses notes from a <u>major</u> or a <u>minor scale</u> — and they're the <u>most important</u> ones to learn, but there are a few other <u>weirdy scales</u> that you need to know about too. And <u>modes</u>. They're very odd.

## Modes Follow Different Patterns of Tones and Semitones

Modes are just like playing the notes of a scale, but starting on different notes.

1) The most common mode is the one you get by playing a major scale (e.g. C major — just play the white notes on a keyboard from C to C). The pattern is *tone-tone-semitone-tone-tone-tone-semitone*.

2) Another mode can be formed by playing the notes of the same major scale, starting from the <u>second note</u>, e.g. D to D:

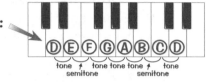

3) Starting from the third note gives you another mode...

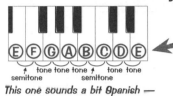

This one sounds a bit Spanish — it's used a lot in flamenco music.

4) ...<u>and so on</u>. Each forms its own semitone / tone pattern and they all have different names, but you don't need to know them — it's more important that you <u>know what they sound like</u> (e.g. it's handy to know that playing the white notes starting from G forms a mode that sounds quite bluesy).

5) Modes are used in all the solos on the Miles Davis album "Kinda Blue". Worth a listen, whether jazz is your bag or not. Guitarists like Joe Satriani use modes too. *(If you ever go to guitar school, you'll learn loads about this stuff.)*

## Pentatonic Scales are Used a lot in Folk and Rock Music

Pentatonic scales use <u>five</u> notes. They're really easy to compose with, because there are <u>no semitone steps</u> — <u>most combinations</u> of notes sound fine. There are <u>two types</u> of pentatonic scale.

1) The <u>major pentatonic</u> uses notes 1, 2, 3, 5 and 6 of a <u>major</u> scale.

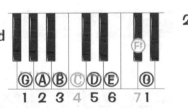

2) The <u>minor pentatonic</u> uses notes 1, 3, 4, 5 and 7 of the <u>natural minor</u> scale.

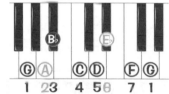

## Whole Tone and Chromatic Scales Sound Spooky

### WHOLE TONE SCALES

Whole tone scales are pretty simple to remember — <u>every step is a tone</u>. From bottom to top there are only <u>seven notes</u> in a whole tone scale.

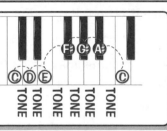

### CHROMATIC SCALES

Chromatic scales are fairly easy too. On a keyboard you play <u>every white and black note</u> until you get up to an octave above the note you started with. From bottom to top there are <u>thirteen notes</u>. Basically <u>every step</u> of a chromatic scale is <u>a semitone</u>.

## I'd like a pentatonic with ice and a slice...

You might be wondering <u>why</u> you need to know all of this. I'll tell you. You <u>could</u> get a piece of music in your <u>listening</u> that's written in a <u>mode</u> or one of the other <u>scales</u>. And you could get <u>asked</u> what kind of scale it's written with. OK, it *might* not happen — but if it does and if you know this stuff you'll <u>get marks</u>.

# Intervals

No — not the break at half-time when everyone rushes out for an <u>ice-cream</u>. The musical kind.

## An Interval is the Gap Between Two Notes

An interval is the posh <u>musical word</u> for the <u>gap</u> or <u>distance</u> between <u>two notes</u>.
Notes <u>close together</u> make <u>small</u> intervals. Notes <u>further apart</u> make <u>larger</u> intervals.
There are <u>two ways</u> of playing an interval.

**MELODIC INTERVAL**
When one note <u>jumps</u> up or down to
another note, you get a <u>melodic interval</u>.

ASCENDING interval   DESCENDING interval

**HARMONIC INTERVAL**
When <u>two notes</u> are played at the <u>same
time</u>, they make a <u>harmonic interval</u>.

## An Interval has Two Parts to its Name...

1) A <u>NUMBER</u>

## an augmented fifth

2) A <u>DESCRIPTION</u>

## The Number Tells You How Many Notes the Interval Covers

1) You get the number by counting up the stave from the bottom note to the
top note. You <u>include</u> the bottom and top notes in your counting.

2) C to E is a <u>third</u> because it covers <u>three letter names</u> — C, D and E.

3) C to F is a <u>fourth</u> because it covers <u>four letter names</u> — C, D, E and F.

4) The number of an interval is sometimes called the <u>interval quantity</u>.

The "description" bit is covered
at the top of the next page...

The interval between
G and D is a <u>fifth</u>.

G A B C D
1 2 3 4 5

An interval covering <u>eight letters</u> —
say A to A — is called an <u>octave</u>.
It's just got one name — it doesn't
follow the two-part name rule.

The interval between
D and F sharp is a <u>third</u>.

D E F♯
1 2 3

# Intervals

## The Description Tells You How the Interval Sounds

The <u>description</u> tells you what the interval <u>sounds like</u>. There are <u>five names</u> for the five main sounds.

> perfect    major    minor    diminished    augmented

1) To work out the <u>description part</u> of an interval's name, think of the <u>lower note</u> of the interval as the <u>first</u> note of a <u>major scale</u>.

2) If the top note of the interval is part of that major scale it's either <u>perfect</u> or <u>major</u>:

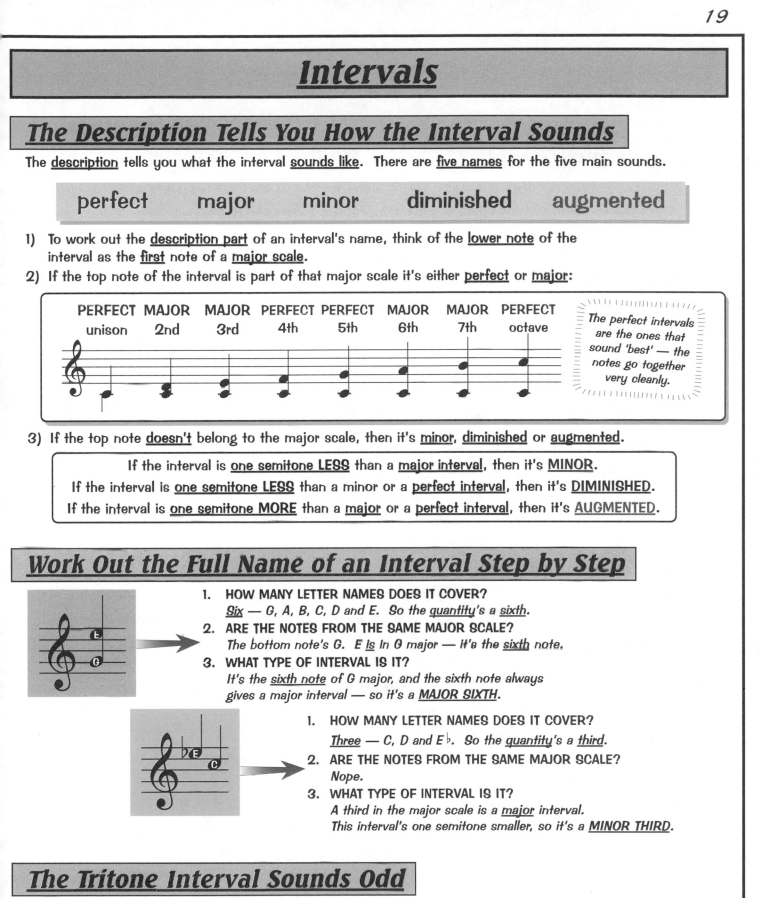

| PERFECT | MAJOR | MAJOR | PERFECT | PERFECT | MAJOR | MAJOR | PERFECT |
| unison | 2nd | 3rd | 4th | 5th | 6th | 7th | octave |

*The perfect intervals are the ones that sound 'best' — the notes go together very cleanly.*

3) If the top note <u>doesn't</u> belong to the major scale, then it's <u>minor</u>, <u>diminished</u> or <u>augmented</u>.

> If the interval is <u>one semitone LESS</u> than a <u>major interval</u>, then it's <u>MINOR</u>.
>
> If the interval is <u>one semitone LESS</u> than a minor or a <u>perfect interval</u>, then it's <u>DIMINISHED</u>.
>
> If the interval is <u>one semitone MORE</u> than a <u>major</u> or a <u>perfect interval</u>, then it's <u>AUGMENTED</u>.

## Work Out the Full Name of an Interval Step by Step

1. **HOW MANY LETTER NAMES DOES IT COVER?**
   *<u>Six</u> — G, A, B, C, D and E. So the <u>quantity</u>'s a <u>sixth</u>.*
2. **ARE THE NOTES FROM THE SAME MAJOR SCALE?**
   *The bottom note's G. E <u>is</u> in G major — it's the <u>sixth</u> note.*
3. **WHAT TYPE OF INTERVAL IS IT?**
   *It's the <u>sixth note</u> of G major, and the sixth note always gives a major interval — so it's a <u>MAJOR SIXTH</u>.*

1. **HOW MANY LETTER NAMES DOES IT COVER?**
   *<u>Three</u> — C, D and E♭. So the <u>quantity</u>'s a <u>third</u>.*
2. **ARE THE NOTES FROM THE SAME MAJOR SCALE?**
   *Nope.*
3. **WHAT TYPE OF INTERVAL IS IT?**
   *A third in the major scale is a <u>major</u> interval. This interval's one semitone smaller, so it's a <u>MINOR THIRD</u>.*

## The Tritone Interval Sounds Odd

1) The tritone is an interval of <u>three tones</u>. It's <u>dissonant</u> — i.e. it sounds a bit awkward, some would say horrible. It's used in some twentieth century Western art music.

2) <u>Diminished fifths</u> (e.g. G to D♭) and <u>augmented fourths</u> (e.g. G to C♯) are both <u>tritones</u>.

3) Try playing some, so you know what they <u>sound</u> like.

## Have you got an interval or an outerval...

The tritone interval used to be called '<u>The Devil's Interval</u>' — it's supposed to be unlucky. It's used somewhere in the Blackadder theme tune actually. Kinda appropriate I guess.

# Revision Summary

*I hope you're hungry — I've got some delicious Revision Summary questions for you, fresh out of the oven. Once you've got on top of these, you can sit back and feel smug. But only when you can answer them <u>without</u> looking back at the section...*

1) How many notes are there in a major scale? How many notes are there in a minor scale?

2) Write out the names of the notes of a scale in words, numbers and Roman numerals.

3) Write down the tone-semitone pattern for a major scale.

4) Which major scale only uses the white notes on the keyboard?

5) Why do all the other major scales have black notes?

6) What does a key signature tell you?

7) What's wrong with this key signature?

8) How do you find the 'relative minor' of a major scale?

9) How do you find the 'relative major' of a minor scale?

10) D major has two sharps — F, and C. What's the key signature of the relative minor?

11) What are the three different types of minor scale called?

12) Write out A minor in each of the three types of minor scale and label the tone and semitone gaps.

13) How many major scales are there altogether?

14) How many minor scales are there altogether?

15) The circle of fifths starts with C major. Write down all the major scales on the circle, in order, starting with C.

16) Why do the key signatures on the circle of fifths change from sharps to flats at the top?

17) What's a pentatonic scale? What types of music do you find pentatonic scales in a lot?

18) What are the notes in G major pentatonic?

19) What are the notes in A minor pentatonic?

20) What's a chromatic scale? How many notes are there in a chromatic scale?

21) What's a whole tone scale?

22) Write out two common modes.

23) What's the difference between a melodic and a harmonic interval?

24) Give the name and number of each of these intervals:

a) A to C

b) B to F♯

c) C to B♭

d) D to A♭

25) What's a tritone?

# Chords — The Basics

A <u>chord</u> is at least two notes played together. Chords are great for writing <u>accompaniments</u>.
In fact, no chords, no accompaniments.

## Only Some Instruments Play Chords

Don't play chords.

1) A lot of instruments only play <u>one note at a time</u> — flutes, recorders, trumpets, clarinets, trombones... You can't play a chord with one note, so these instruments <u>don't</u> play chords.

2) You can <u>only</u> play chords on <u>instruments</u> that play <u>more than one</u> note at a time. <u>Keyboards</u> and <u>guitars</u> are both great for playing chords — you can easily play several notes together.

Do play chords.

3) Other <u>stringed instruments</u> like violins and cellos can play chords, but <u>not</u> very easily, so chords are only played from time to time.

## Some Chords Sound Great, Others Sound Awful

1) The notes of some chords go together really well — like apple pie and ice-cream.

Nice-sounding chords are called <u>CONCORDS</u>.

2) Other chords have <u>clashing notes</u> <u>which disagree</u> — more like apple pie and pickled eggs.

Horrible-sounding chords are called <u>DISCORDS</u>.

## The Best-Sounding Chords are Called Triads

1) You can play <u>any</u> set of notes and make a chord — but most of them sound <u>awful</u>.
2) An <u>easy</u>, <u>reliable</u> way of getting nice-sounding chords is to play <u>triads</u>.
3) Triads are chords made up of three notes, with <u>set intervals</u> between them.
4) Once you know the intervals, you can easily play <u>dozens</u> of decent chords.

### HOW TO MAKE A TRIAD...

1) On a piano, start with any white note — this is called the <u>root note</u>. You <u>build</u> the triad <u>from the root</u>.

2) Count the root as 'first' and the next white note to the <u>right</u>, as 'second'. The <u>third</u> note you reach is the <u>third</u> — the middle note of the triad.

3) Keep counting up and you get to the <u>fifth</u> — the final note of the triad.

4) The intervals between the notes are <u>thirds</u>.

5) If the root note's a <u>B</u>, then you end up with a <u>B triad</u>. If the root note's a <u>C</u>, you end up with a <u>C triad</u>.

6) You can build triads on black notes too, so long as the intervals between notes are <u>thirds</u>.

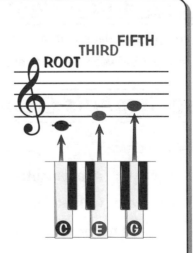

ROOT   THIRD  FIFTH

Ⓒ  Ⓔ  Ⓖ

## Chords — your music teacher's favourite trousers...

This looks like another of those pages where you might know it all already. Still, it won't hurt to read through again and <u>check</u> you <u>really do</u> know it all. The rest of this section gets tricky so enjoy the easy stuff while it lasts...

# Triads

There's more than one type of triad...

## Triads Use Major and Minor Thirds

1) All triads have an interval of a <u>third</u> between each pair of notes.

2) The intervals can be <u>major</u> or <u>minor thirds</u>.

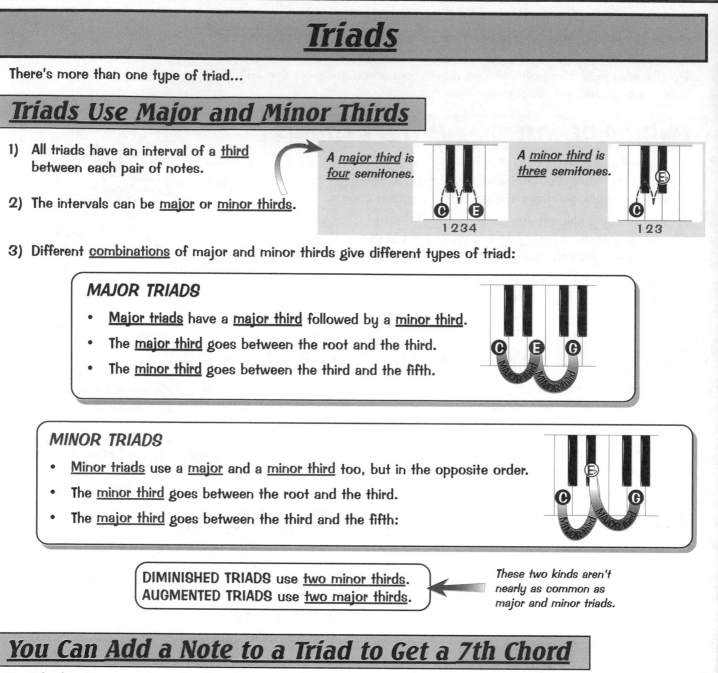

A <u>major third</u> is <u>four</u> semitones.

A <u>minor third</u> is <u>three</u> semitones.

3) Different <u>combinations</u> of major and minor thirds give different types of triad:

**MAJOR TRIADS**

- <u>Major triads</u> have a <u>major third</u> followed by a <u>minor third</u>.
- The <u>major third</u> goes between the root and the third.
- The <u>minor third</u> goes between the third and the fifth.

**MINOR TRIADS**

- <u>Minor triads</u> use a <u>major</u> and a <u>minor third</u> too, but in the opposite order.
- The <u>minor third</u> goes between the root and the third.
- The <u>major third</u> goes between the third and the fifth:

DIMINISHED TRIADS use <u>two minor thirds</u>.
AUGMENTED TRIADS use <u>two major thirds</u>.

*These two kinds aren't nearly as common as major and minor triads.*

## You Can Add a Note to a Triad to Get a 7th Chord

1) <u>7th chords</u> are triads with a fourth note added — the <u>seventh</u> note above the root.

2) The interval between the root and the 7th can be <u>major seventh</u> or a <u>minor seventh</u> — see P.19.

## These Symbols Stand for Chords

C = C major

Caug or C+ = augmented C chord

C7 = C major with added minor 7th

Cmaj7 = C major with added major 7th

Cm = C minor

Cdim or C- or Co = diminished C chord

Cm7 = C minor with added minor 7th

Cm maj7 = C minor with added major 7th

For chords other than C just change the <u>first letter</u> to show the <u>root note</u>.

## Does this look hard — it's easy when you triad...

Those symbols come up all the time in pop music — if you play the guitar or play in a band you need to learn them <u>right now</u>. And even if you only ever play baroque music on period instruments you'd <u>still</u> better learn 'em — they're really useful as shorthand when you're talking about chords.

# Fitting Chords to a Melody

There are some basic rules about fitting chords to a melody:

*No.1: All the notes in the chords have got to be in the same key as the notes in the melody.*

## The Melody and Chords Must Be in the Same Key

1) A melody that's composed in a certain key <u>sticks</u> to that key.
2) The chords used to <u>harmonise with</u> the melody have got to be in the <u>same key</u> or it'll sound <u>awful</u>.
3) As a <u>general rule</u> each chord in a harmony should <u>include</u> the note it's accompanying,
   e.g. a <u>C</u> could be accompanied by a <u>C chord</u> (C, E, G), an <u>F chord</u> (F, A, C) or an <u>A minor chord</u> (A, C, E).

## There's a Chord for Every Note in the Scale

You can make a whole bunch of triads using the notes of <u>major</u> and <u>minor</u> scales as the <u>roots</u>. <u>Every note</u> of <u>every chord</u>, not just the root, has to belong to the scale. This is how <u>C major</u> looks if you turn it into chords:

> *The odd accidental or ornament in a different key is OK — <u>see p.27</u>.*

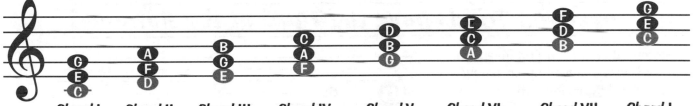

| Chord I | Chord II | Chord III | Chord IV | Chord V | Chord VI | Chord VII | Chord I |
|---------|----------|-----------|----------|---------|----------|-----------|---------|
| Tonic | Supertonic | Mediant | Subdominant | Dominant | Submediant | Leading Note | Tonic |

1) Chords I, IV and V are <u>major triads</u>. They sound <u>bright and cheery</u>.
2) Chords II, III and VI are <u>minor triads</u>. They sound more <u>gloomy</u>.
3) Chord VII is a <u>diminished triad</u>. It sounds really <u>different</u> from the major and minor chords. Another name for Chord VII is the <u>Leading Note Chord</u> — it sounds a bit like it should lead on to another chord.
4) Chords built on <u>any</u> major scale, not just C major, follow the <u>same pattern</u>.

## The Primary Chords are Most Useful

1) The three major chords, <u>I</u>, <u>IV</u> and <u>V</u>, are the <u>most important</u> in <u>any</u> key. They're called <u>primary chords</u>.
2) Between them, the primary chords can harmonise with <u>any note</u> in the scale.
3) This is how it works in <u>C major</u>:

| NOTE | C | | D | E | F | | G | | A | B |
|------|---|---|---|---|---|---|---|---|---|---|
| GOES WITH | Chord I | Chord IV | Chord V | Chord I | Chord IV | | Chord I | Chord V | Chord IV | Chord V |
| | G | C | D | G | C | | G | D | C | D |
| | E | A | B | E | A | | E | B | A | B |
| | C | F | G | C | F | | C | G | F | G |

## Minor Chords Make Harmony More Interesting

1) Primary chords (amazingly amazing as they are) can get a bit <u>boring</u> to listen to after a while.
2) Composers often mix in a few of the other chords — <u>II</u>, <u>III</u>, <u>VI</u> or <u>VII</u> — for a <u>change</u>.
3) Instead of just having endless major chords, you get a mixture of minor and diminished chords too. <u>Much</u> more interesting.

## Go on, write a harmony, you know you want to...

Actually, you can't turn <u>any</u> scale into chords. You can't turn a <u>fish scale</u> or a <u>lizard scale</u> into chords. But any major or minor scale you can turn into chords. And once you've done that you can fit them to your melody. Try the major chords first, then liven things up with some minor chords.

# Inversions

Inverting triads means changing the order of the notes.  It helps make accompaniments a bit more varied.

## Triads with the Root at the Bottom are in Root Position

These triads are all in root position — the root note's at the bottom.

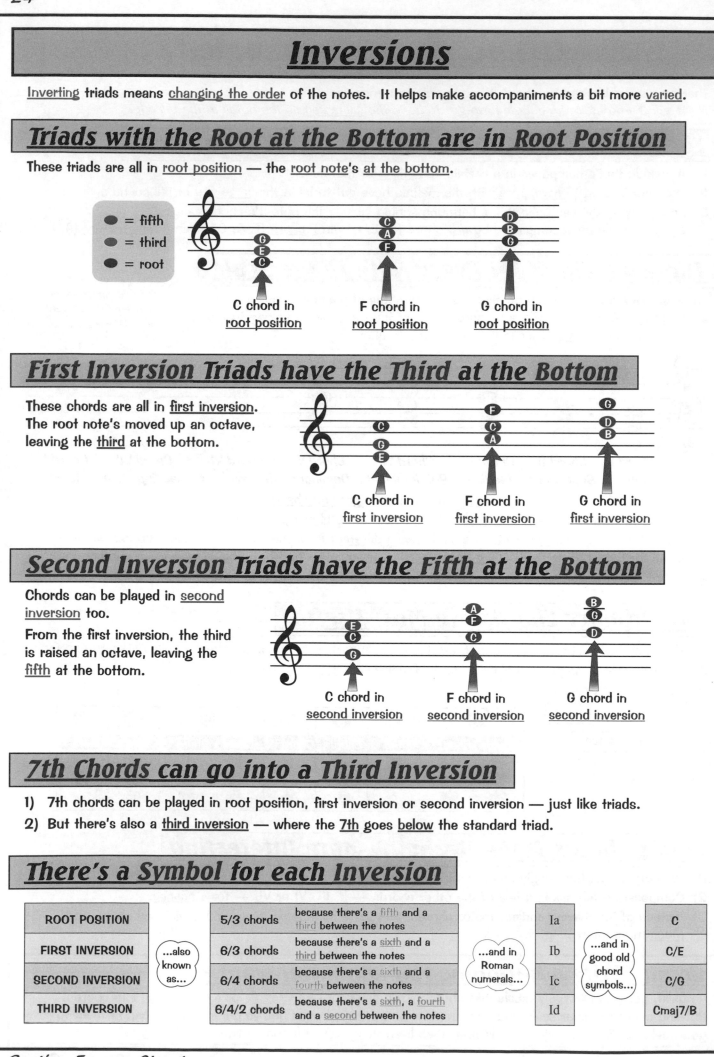

● = fifth
● = third
● = root

C chord in root position

F chord in root position

G chord in root position

## First Inversion Triads have the Third at the Bottom

These chords are all in first inversion. The root note's moved up an octave, leaving the third at the bottom.

C chord in first inversion

F chord in first inversion

G chord in first inversion

## Second Inversion Triads have the Fifth at the Bottom

Chords can be played in second inversion too.

From the first inversion, the third is raised an octave, leaving the fifth at the bottom.

C chord in second inversion

F chord in second inversion

G chord in second inversion

## 7th Chords can go into a Third Inversion

1) 7th chords can be played in root position, first inversion or second inversion — just like triads.
2) But there's also a third inversion — where the 7th goes below the standard triad.

## There's a Symbol for each Inversion

| | | | | | | |
|---|---|---|---|---|---|---|
| ROOT POSITION | ...also known as... | 5/3 chords | because there's a fifth and a third between the notes | ...and in Roman numerals... | Ia | ...and in good old chord symbols... | C |
| FIRST INVERSION | | 6/3 chords | because there's a sixth and a third between the notes | | Ib | | C/E |
| SECOND INVERSION | | 6/4 chords | because there's a sixth and a fourth between the notes | | Ic | | C/G |
| THIRD INVERSION | | 6/4/2 chords | because there's a sixth, a fourth and a second between the notes | | Id | | Cmaj7/B |

*Section Four — Chords*

# *Inversions*

So now you know what inversions <u>are</u>.  Now get to grips with what to <u>do</u> with them too...

## *Inversions are Handy for Moving Between Chords*

When you play chords one after another, it sounds <u>nicer</u> if the notes move <u>smoothly</u> from one chord to the next.  Inversions help to smooth out any rough patches...

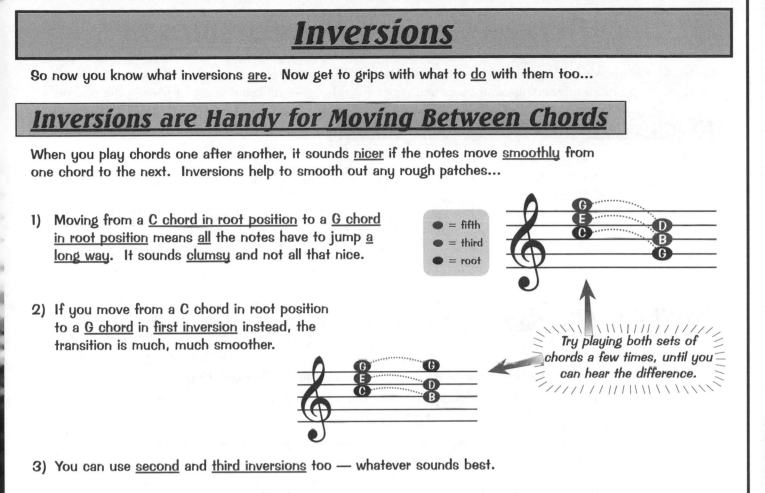

1) Moving from a <u>C chord in root position</u> to a <u>G chord in root position</u> means <u>all</u> the notes have to jump <u>a long way</u>.  It sounds <u>clumsy</u> and not all that nice.

● = fifth
● = third
● = root

2) If you move from a C chord in root position to a <u>G chord</u> in <u>first inversion</u> instead, the transition is much, much smoother.

*Try playing both sets of chords a few times, until you can hear the difference.*

3) You can use <u>second</u> and <u>third inversions</u> too — whatever sounds best.

## *Unscramble the Inversion to work out the Root Note*

This isn't exactly a life-saving skill.  But it's <u>dead useful</u>...
If you come across an inverted chord you can <u>work out</u> which is the <u>root note</u>.  Once you know that, and you know what <u>key</u> you're in, you can tell whether it's chord IV, VII, II or whatever.

1) Basically you have to turn the chord back into a <u>root position triad</u>.

2) Shuffle the order of the notes around until there's a <u>third interval</u> between each one.

3) When the notes are arranged in <u>thirds</u>, the root will <u>always</u> be at the <u>bottom</u>.

B to D is a **THIRD**, but D to G is a **FOURTH**.
You need to <u>move the G</u> to find the root chord.

G to B is a **THIRD** so the G goes here — <u>G</u>'s the <u>root note</u>.

4) There are no sharps or flats in the key signature, so the piece is in C major.
G's the fifth note of C major, so this is <u>chord V</u>.

## *Unscramble inversions — go back to your roots...*

Well, if those two pages haven't made your ears <u>bleed</u> with confusion, you're either superhuman, subhuman or a music genius.  There's a lot to take in, so go over it one bit at a time till you <u>really</u> get it.

# Different Ways of Playing Chords

So far, all the chords in this section have been written as three notes played together. It sounds a bit dull. To make things more interesting composers use chord figurations — different ways of playing the chords.

## Block Chords are the Most Basic

This is probably the easiest way to play chords. The notes of each chord are played all together and then held until the next chord.

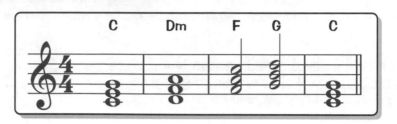

## Rhythmic Chords Give You Harmony and Rhythm

1) Rhythmic chords are chords played to a funky rhythm.

2) You play all the notes of each chord at the same time, like you do for block chords.

3) You don't hold the notes though — you play them to a rhythm that repeats in each bar.

4) Rhythm guitar and keyboards often play rhythmic chords.

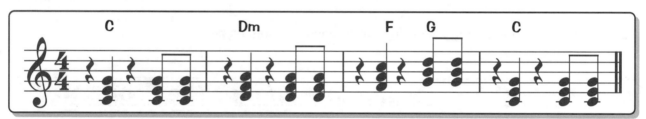

## In Broken and Arpeggiated Chords Notes are Separate

An accompaniment doesn't have to have chords with all the notes played at once. You can play the notes separately too.

Here's one way of doing it — it goes root, fifth, third, root.

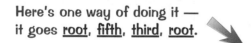

This pattern was dead popular around the time Mozart was alive (last half of the 1700s). It's called Alberti bass after the bloke who made it up (Domenico Alberti) — it goes root, fifth, third, fifth.

The notes of a chord are sometimes played in order (root, third, fifth, root) going up or coming down. This is called an arpeggio (are-pej-jee-o).

## Alberti's Haddock doesn't have quite the same ring...

You know when you get chord symbols over the music... well, when that happens, it basically means you can play the chords any way you like. Try out all the ways of playing chords on this page and think about using them in your compositions — don't get stuck with boring old block chords.

# _Using Decoration to Vary the Harmony_

If you want to <u>liven things up</u> in a harmony you can add a sprinkle of <u>melodic decoration</u> —
a fancy way of saying <u>bung a few extra notes in</u>.

## Melodic Decoration Adds Notes to the Tune

1) <u>Decorative notes</u> are <u>short notes</u> that create <u>fleeting clashes</u> or <u>dissonance</u> with the accompanying chord.  They make things sound <u>less bland</u>.

2) Decoration that belongs to the key of the melody is called <u>DIATONIC</u>.

3) Decoration that <u>doesn't</u> belong to the key, e.g. F♯ in C major, is called <u>CHROMATIC</u>.

4) There are <u>four</u> main ways of adding melodic decoration.

### 1) Auxiliary Notes are Higher or Lower than the Notes Either Side

1) An auxiliary note is either a <u>semitone</u> or <u>tone</u> <u>above</u> or <u>below</u> the notes either side.

2) The two notes before and after the auxiliary are always the <u>same pitch</u>, and always belong to the accompanying chord.

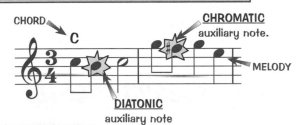

### 2) Passing Notes Link the Notes Before and After

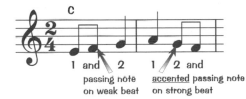

1) A passing note <u>links</u> the notes before and after. Both of them have to belong to the accompanying chord.

2) They're usually put on <u>weak beats</u>.  When they <u>are</u> on the strong beat they're called '<u>accented passing notes</u>'.

### 3) Appoggiaturas Clash with the Chord

1) An appoggiatura <u>clashes</u> with the accompanying chord.

2) The note <u>before</u> it is usually quite a <u>jump</u> away.

3) The note <u>after</u> the appoggiatura is always <u>just above</u> or <u>below</u>.  It's called the <u>resolution</u>.  The <u>resolution</u> has to be from the <u>accompanying chord</u>.

4) Appoggiaturas usually fall on a <u>strong beat</u>, so the resolution note falls on a <u>weaker beat</u>.

_See P.12 for more on appoggiaturas._

### 4) Suspensions Clash then Go Back to Harmonising

A suspension is a series of three notes called the <u>preparation</u>, <u>suspension</u> and <u>resolution</u>.

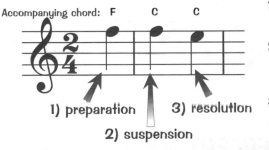

1) The <u>preparation</u> note belongs to the accompanying chord. It's usually on a weak beat.

2) The <u>suspension</u> is the <u>same pitch</u> as the preparation note. It's played at the same time as a <u>chord change</u>.  It <u>doesn't go</u> with the new chord, so you get <u>dissonance</u>.

3) The <u>resolution</u> note moves up or down (usually down) from the suspension to a note in the accompanying chord.  This <u>resolves</u> the dissonance — everything sounds lovely again.

## _Passing notes is so juvenile..._

The best way to get the hang of melodic decorations is to <u>try them out</u> for yourself when you're composing.  And once you've got the hang of them, use them — you're likely to get <u>higher marks</u>.

# Phrases and Cadences

Notes in a melody fall into 'phrases' just like the words in a story fall into phrases and sentences. A cadence is the movement from the second-last chord to the last chord of a phrase — to finish the phrase off nicely.

## A Phrase is like a Musical 'Sentence'

There should be clear phrases in any melody. A tune without phrases would sound odd — just like a story with no sentences wouldn't make much sense.

1) Phrases are usually two or four bars long.

2) Phrases are sometimes marked with a curved line called a phrase mark, that goes above the stave. Not all music has phrase marks but the phrases are always there. Don't confuse phrase marks and slurs. A phrase mark doesn't change how you play the notes.

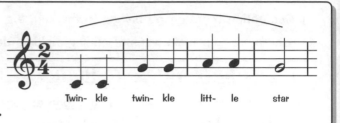

Twin- kle  twin- kle  litt- le  star

## Cadences Emphasise the End of a Phrase

1) A cadence is the shift between the second-last chord and the last chord in a phrase.

2) The effect you get from shifting between the two chords works like a comma or a full stop. It underlines the end of the phrase and gets you ready for the next one.

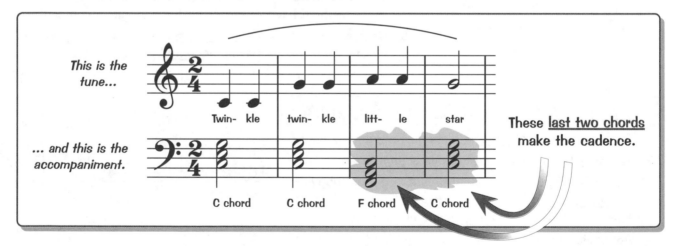

*This is the tune...*

Twin- kle  twin- kle  litt- le  star

*... and this is the accompaniment.*

C chord   C chord   F chord   C chord

These last two chords make the cadence.

## There are Four Types of Cadence

These pairs of chords are only cadences when they come at the end of a phrase. Anywhere else in a phrase, they're just chords.

| Second Last Chord | Last Chord | | Cadence |
|---|---|---|---|
| Chord V | Chord I | → | PERFECT |
| Chord IV | Chord I | → | PLAGAL |
| Chord I, II or IV | Chord V | → | IMPERFECT |
| Chord V | any except Chord I | → | INTERRUPTED |

More on these over there...

# Cadences

It's no good just knowing the names of the different cadences. You need to know what they're used for.

## Perfect and Plagal Cadences Work Like Full Stops

1) A PERFECT CADENCE makes a piece of music feel finished or complete.

2) It goes from Chord V to Chord I — in C major that's a G chord to a C chord.

3) This is how a perfect cadence goes at the end of 'Twinkle, Twinkle, Little Star':

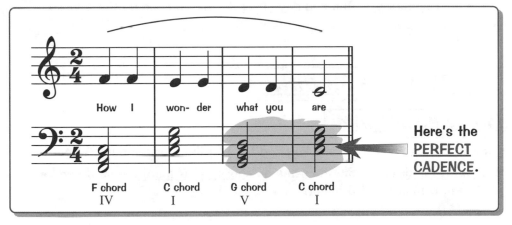

Here's the PERFECT CADENCE.

A PLAGAL CADENCE sounds really different from a perfect cadence but it has a similar effect — it makes a piece of music sound finished.

A plagal cadence in C major is an F chord (IV) to a C chord (I). Play it and see what it sounds like. The plagal cadence gets used at the end of lots of hymns — it's sometimes called the 'Amen' cadence.

## Imperfect and Interrupted Cadences are Like Commas

Imperfect and interrupted cadences are used to end phrases but not at the end of a piece. They work like commas — they feel like a resting point but not an ending.

An IMPERFECT CADENCE most commonly goes from chord I, II or IV to V. Here's one going from chord I to chord V at the end of the third line of 'Twinkle, Twinkle':

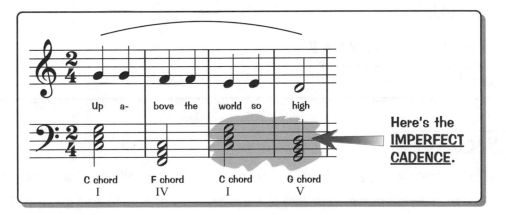

Here's the IMPERFECT CADENCE.

In an INTERRUPTED CADENCE chord V can go to any chord except I. You expect it to go to chord I — so it sounds "interrupted". In C major an interrupted cadence may go from a G chord (V) to an Am chord (VI).

## The seventh plagal was the plagal of frogs...

This is another of those topics that isn't going to make much sense unless you sit down at a keyboard and have a go. Read through again, and play the cadences until you can hear the differences between them. And then learn it all off by heart. Off by heart I said. Not half-hearted. Learn it all.

# Modulation

Most of the notes in a piece of music come from one key — but to vary the tune or harmony you can <u>modulate</u> — <u>change key</u>. It can happen just once, or a few times in a piece. It's up to the composer.

## The Starting Key is Called 'Home'

1) The key a piece <u>starts out in</u> is called the <u>home key</u>.
2) If the music's modulated it goes into a <u>different key</u>.
3) The change of key is only <u>temporary</u>. The key <u>goes back</u> to the home key after a while.
4) However much a piece modulates, it usually <u>ends</u> in the home key.

## There are Two Ways to Modulate

### 1) Modulation by Pivot Chord

1) A pivot chord is a chord that's in the home key <u>and</u> the key the music modulates to.
2) <u>Chord V</u> (G, B, D) in <u>C major</u> is exactly the same as <u>chord I</u> in <u>G major</u> — so it can be used to <u>pivot</u> between C major and G major.
3) Sometimes, the <u>key signature</u> changes to show the new key.
   More often, <u>accidentals</u> are written in the music where they're needed.

The home key here is <u>C</u>. At the end of the <u>first bar</u> the accompaniment uses the chord <u>G, B, D</u> to pivot into G major:

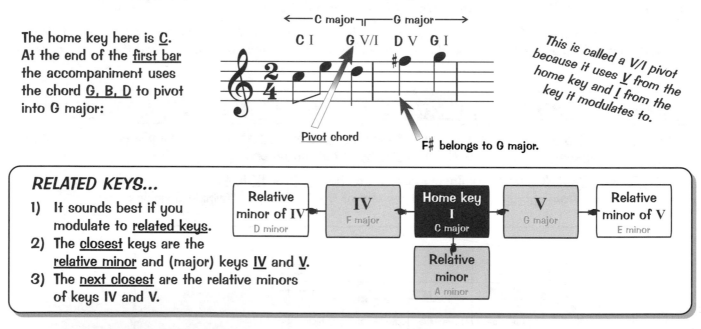

← C major ⌐⌐ G major →

C I    G V/I    D V    G I

Pivot chord

*This is called a V/I pivot because it uses V from the home key and I from the key it modulates to.*

F♯ belongs to G major.

**RELATED KEYS...**

1) It sounds best if you modulate to <u>related keys</u>.
2) The <u>closest</u> keys are the <u>relative minor</u> and (major) keys <u>IV</u> and <u>V</u>.
3) The <u>next closest</u> are the relative minors of keys IV and V.

| Relative minor of IV<br>D minor | IV<br>F major | Home key<br>I<br>C major | V<br>G major | Relative minor of V<br>E minor |

Relative minor
A minor

### 2) Abrupt Modulation

1) In abrupt modulation there's <u>no pivot chord</u>, and no other preparation either. It just happens.
2) Often the modulation is between two keys just <u>one semitone apart</u>, e.g. from <u>C major</u> to <u>C♯ major</u>.
3) <u>Pop songs</u> often modulate <u>up</u> one semitone. It creates a <u>sudden,</u> <u>dramatic effect</u> — it's meant to give the music an <u>excited</u>, <u>uplifting</u> feeling.

## You can choose related keys but you can't choose your family...

If you see <u>accidentals</u> it often means the music's modulated, but <u>not always</u>.
The accidental could also be there because: 1) the music's written in a <u>minor key</u> — harmonic or melodic (see P.15); or 2) the composer fancied a spot of <u>chromatic</u> decoration (see P.27).

# Texture

Here's one last way composers vary the harmony — by changing the <u>texture</u>. Texture's quite a bizarre word to use about music — what it means is how the chords and melody are <u>woven together</u>.

## Monophonic Music is the Simplest

In <u>monophonic</u> music there's <u>no</u> harmony — just one line of tune.

## Polyphonic Music Weaves Tunes Together

<u>Polyphonic</u> music gives quite a complex effect because there's <u>more than one tune</u> being played at once.

*It's sometimes called* **CONTRAPUNTAL** *music too.*

## In Homophonic Music, the Parts Move Together

If the lines of music move at more or less the <u>same time</u>, it's <u>homophonic</u> music. Melody and chords (chordal music) is a good example.

Melody

Accompaniment

## In Heterophonic Music the Instruments Share the Tune

Flute

Oboe

In heterophonic music there's <u>one tune</u>. <u>All</u> the instruments play it, but with <u>variations</u>.

## These are Other Ways of Varying Texture

**SOLO**
one voice or instrument on its own

**DUET**
2-part piece

**TRIO**
3-part piece

**QUARTET**
4-part piece

**UNISON**
all voices or instruments playing the same notes

**TUTTI**
all instruments or voices playing at the same time

**DOUBLING**
one part playing exactly the same notes as another

**DESCANT**
part that runs along higher than the main melody

## The Polyphonics — just East of Micronesia...

It's hard talking about texture — a bit like trying to describe a smell... If you need to write about <u>texture</u> in your listening test, these are handy words to use: smooth, dense, thick, heavy, light, thin... Go and get a <u>thesaurus</u> and scribble a few more words down, just in case.

# Revision Summary

There's a lot to remember in this section: all four types of triad, all four types of inversion for triads, all those cadences, all the different ways of using decoration with chords, what all those blah-phonic words mean, _and_ modulation. It's a right _old hairy mammoth_ of a section and there's no way you'll get it all down in one mouthful. Chop the fearsome beast into tiny bite-size portions, and glue each one firmly to the cavern of your brain before you go attempt the next one. You'll know you've minced it fine enough when you can answer all these questions easily _without_ looking back.

1) What's a chord?
2) Why can't you play a chord on a clarinet?
3) What do you call chords with:
   a) clashing notes     b) notes that sound good together?
4) How many notes are there in a triad?
5) The first note of a triad's called the root. What are the other two notes called?
6) What do you call a triad with B♭ as the root note?
7) How is a major third interval different from a minor third?
8) What are the two most common types of triad? Describe how you make each one.
9) What are the two less popular (_less loved, sniff_) triads called?
10) What makes a 7th chord different from a triad?
11) Write down the letter symbols for these chords:
   a) G major     b) A minor     c) A minor with a major 7th
   d) D diminished triad     e) G augmented triad
12) How can you be fairly sure a note will sound good with a chord?
13) Draw the scale of G major on a stave, then build a triad on each note. (_Don't forget the F sharps._)
14) Which three chords of any major or minor scale are known as the 'primary' chords?
15) What's so special about primary chords?
16) Write out the notes of the three primary chords in C major, G major and D major.
17) Why don't composers use primary chords all the time?
18) Where do the root, third and fifth go in:
   a) a first inversion chord     b) a second inversion chord?
19) What kind of chords can have a third inversion?
20) Are these chords in root position, first inversion, second inversion or third inversion?
   a) 6/4     b) C/E     c) IVa     d) 6/4/2
21) What's the point of using inversions?
22) How do you work out the root note of an inverted chord?
23) Name and describe four different chord figurations.
24) What's melodic decoration?
25) What's the difference between a 'diatonic' decoration and a 'chromatic' decoration?
26) Explain the following terms:
   a) auxiliary note     b) passing note     c) an appoggiatura     d) a suspension
27) Write a one-sentence definition of a musical phrase.
28) What job does a cadence do in a phrase?
29) How many chords make up a cadence?
30) Write down the four different types of cadence and which chords you can use to make each one.
31) What's the difference between perfect and plagal cadences, and interrupted and imperfect cadences?
32) What's modulation? Name and describe the two different types.
33) Draw a diagram with G major at the centre, showing the most closely related keys.
34) What do people mean when they talk about the 'texture' of music?
35) Explain the difference between monophonic music, homophonic music and polyphonic music.
36) What do you call three musicians playing together? (_this is not a joke_)
37) What's the Italian word used when all the parts are played at the same time?

# How Music's Organised

Music isn't just random notes — it's carefully organised, or at least it's meant to be.
Planning and organising makes music <u>sound better</u>, and makes it <u>easier to write</u>.

## Music Needs Form and Structure

1) Music's got to be organised, or it just sounds like lots of <u>plinky-plonky notes</u>.
2) The <u>most basic</u> bit of organisation is the <u>beats of a bar</u>. The next biggest chunk is the <u>phrasing</u>.
3) The <u>overall shape</u> is called the <u>structure</u> or <u>form</u>.
4) The structure could be, e.g. the <u>verses</u> and <u>chorus</u> in a pop song, or the <u>movements</u> of a symphony.
5) Composers usually <u>plan the structure</u> of a piece of music <u>before</u> they get into the detail.

## Most Musical Plans Use Repetition *Repetition* Repetition ...

1) <u>Repetition</u> means using a <u>musical idea</u> — a chunk of tune — <u>more than once</u>.
2) Repeating bits is a really good way of giving music <u>shape</u>. Once the audience know a tune it works like a <u>landmark</u> — they know where they are when they hear that tune <u>later</u> in the piece. (That's how choruses work, of course.)
3) If you're planning <u>your own</u> piece of music try repeating the best part of the tune.

### ...and *Contrast*

*See P.34 & P.35 for more on repetition and contrast.*

1) Repetition is really important — but <u>constant repetition</u> is <u>boring</u>.
2) Good compositions balance repetition with <u>contrast</u>. The aim is to do something <u>different</u> from the repeated bits to add <u>variety</u>.
3) There's contrast in just about <u>every</u> piece of music.
4) The <u>verse and chorus structure</u> of a pop song is one of the most obvious ways of using contrast.

## If You're Composing, Plan the Structure First

1) Making a <u>musical plan</u> helps to <u>organise</u> your ideas — it's a bit like writing an essay plan.
2) It's OK to <u>design your own</u> musical plan but a lot of people use '<u>tried and tested</u>' plans like the ones described in the rest of this section, because they know they'll work.
3) 'Tried and tested' plans are like <u>templates</u>. The <u>general organisation</u> of your ideas is decided for you — you just need to add the <u>details</u>.

## Learn to Spot the Plan When You're Listening to Music

In your listening exam, you'll need to <u>recognise</u> and <u>write about</u> the <u>basic structure</u> of the music.
To help you work it out, ask yourself these questions as you're listening...

- *Which bits are <u>repeated</u>?*
- *Is there a <u>main idea</u> that gets repeated more than once? How many <u>times</u> do you hear it?*
- *Are there any <u>contrasting ideas</u>? How many? What's different about them?*
- *Is there a special <u>introduction</u> or <u>ending</u> section?*
- *Does the music have a plan similar to a piece you <u>already know</u>?*

## Holst very organised — he always plan it...

The thing nobody mentions about repetition is, it's a lot <u>less effort</u> to repeat a good tune than make up a new one. Bear it in mind if you're a bit lazy like me. The thing nobody mentions about repetition is, it's a lot <u>less effort</u> to repeat a good tune than make up a new one. Bear it in mind if you're a bit lazy like me.

# Binary, Ternary & Rondo Form

The binary, ternary and rondo forms are pretty simple — and what's more, they work.

## Binary Form has Two Sections

1) Binary means something like 'in two parts' — there are two bits to a piece of music in binary form.

2) To make it easier to talk about the two bits you usually call the first one A and the second one B.

3) Each section is repeated. You play A twice, and then B twice — so you end up with AABB.

4) Section B contrasts with section A — the two parts should sound different.

5) The contrast's often made by modulating. (See P.30)

6) The first modulation comes at the end of Section A. At the end of Section B the piece modulates back to the original key.

7) If you start in a major key, modulate to the dominant key (V), e.g. C major to G major.

8) If you start in a minor key, modulate to the relative major, e.g. A minor to C major.

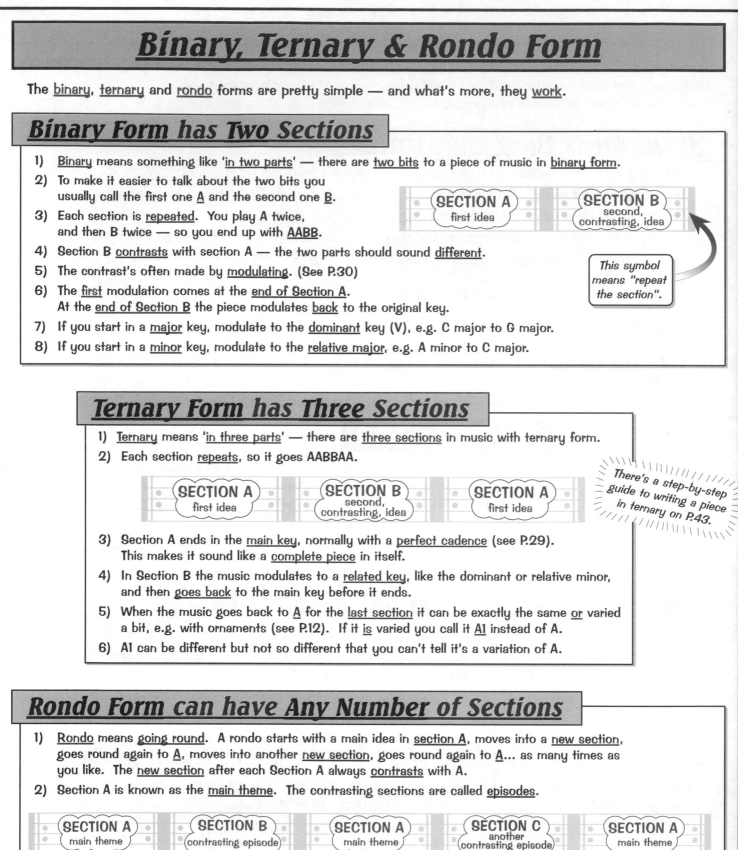

This symbol means "repeat the section".

## Ternary Form has Three Sections

1) Ternary means 'in three parts' — there are three sections in music with ternary form.

2) Each section repeats, so it goes AABBAA.

There's a step-by-step guide to writing a piece in ternary on P.43.

3) Section A ends in the main key, normally with a perfect cadence (see P.29). This makes it sound like a complete piece in itself.

4) In Section B the music modulates to a related key, like the dominant or relative minor, and then goes back to the main key before it ends.

5) When the music goes back to A for the last section it can be exactly the same or varied a bit, e.g. with ornaments (see P.12). If it is varied you call it A1 instead of A.

6) A1 can be different but not so different that you can't tell it's a variation of A.

## Rondo Form can have Any Number of Sections

1) Rondo means going round. A rondo starts with a main idea in section A, moves into a new section, goes round again to A, moves into another new section, goes round again to A... as many times as you like. The new section after each Section A always contrasts with A.

2) Section A is known as the main theme. The contrasting sections are called episodes.

3) The main theme is always in the main key. Each episode tends to modulate to a related key to create contrast.

4) The most important thing to remember is that after every new section, Section A always comes back. It literally does keep 'going round'.

## I'm confused — what's quandary form...

In the listening test, when you're all flushed and panicky, this trick of using letters as shorthand is very handy indeed. As you're listening, put A for the first bit, B for a new bit, A1 for a variation of A... and so on. It's quick and clear — you should end up with a plan of the music that's easy to recognise.

# Variations

Variations are pieces which start with <u>one pattern</u> or tune, and then <u>change it</u> in different ways.
There are <u>two</u> main structures for variation, called "<u>theme and variation</u>" and "<u>ground bass</u>".

## Theme and Variation Form Varies the Melody

1) "<u>Theme</u>" is another name for the <u>main musical idea</u> of a piece.

2) In <u>theme and variation form</u>, the theme's usually a memorable <u>tune</u> — like the James Bond theme.

3) The theme's played <u>first</u>, then there's a short <u>pause</u> before the <u>first variation</u>'s played, then another pause before the next variation. Each variation is a <u>self-contained</u> piece of music. There can be <u>as many</u> or <u>as few</u> variations as the composer wants.

4) Each variation should be a <u>recognisable</u> version of the main theme, but <u>different</u> from all the others.

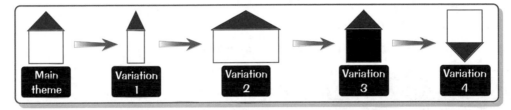

5) Many composers pick an <u>existing</u> tune — like <u>Greensleeves</u> or <u>Twinkle, Twinkle</u> — to use as the theme and then make up their own variations.

---

*You can vary a theme by using any of these <u>techniques</u>.*
<u>Listen</u> *for them in the exam, and <u>use</u> them when you're composing.*

1) <u>Add notes</u> to make the tune more complex — see ornamentation on P.12.

2) <u>Remove</u> notes to <u>simplify</u> the tune.

3) <u>Change</u> the length of the notes. It's called diminution or augmentation — see P.45.

4) a) Turn the melody <u>upside down</u>. This is called melodic <u>inversion</u> — see P.45.

   b) Turn the melody <u>back-to-front</u>. This is called <u>retrograde</u>, e.g. CDEG becomes GEDC.

   c) Turn the melody <u>upside down and back-to-front</u>. This is called <u>retrograde inversion</u>.

5) Add a <u>countermelody</u> — an extra melody over the top of the theme.

6) Change the <u>key</u> (<u>tonality</u>) — from major to minor.

7) Change the <u>tempo</u> — make the theme faster or slower.

8) Change the <u>metre</u> — say, from two beats in a bar to three.

9) <u>Change</u> some or all of the <u>chords</u> in the harmony — see Section 4.

10) <u>Add</u> a different <u>accompaniment pattern</u> to suggest a <u>particular style</u>, e.g. an '<u>oom pa pa</u>' waltz pattern, an off-beat <u>syncopated</u> jazzy rhythm or a classical '<u>alberti bass</u>' pattern (P.26).

---

## Ground Bass Form Varies Ideas Over a Fixed Bass Part

1) <u>Ground bass</u> is a <u>continuous</u> set of variations — there are <u>no pauses</u>.

2) The main theme — called the <u>ground</u> — is a <u>bass line</u> which <u>repeats</u> throughout the piece.

3) <u>Varying melodies</u> and <u>harmonies</u> which become gradually <u>more complex</u> are played <u>over</u> the ground.

4) There are two types of seventeenth century dance that are in ground bass form — the <u>chaconne</u> and <u>passacaglia</u>. They're quite <u>slow</u> and <u>stately</u>.

---

## I hope this themes leth tricky than it looked at first...

Variations are a <u>great starting point</u> for composition. Try borrowing a tune, from your favourite song or something, then compose your own set of variations. Use the ideas from the box to help you think about how to <u>vary</u> the theme. Even better, start off by composing your own theme.

# Basic Structures for Songs

People have been writing songs for thousands of years and they've come up with a fair old number of song structures. What's more a song structure never caused any <u>death</u> or <u>pollution</u>, I don't think.

## Call and Response Sounds like a Conversation

1) A call and response structure has <u>two bits</u> to it:

> Part 1, the <u>CALL</u>, asks a <u>question</u>.    Part 2, the <u>RESPONSE</u>, gives an <u>answer</u>.

2) To give the feeling of question and answer, the <u>call</u> ends on note 5 or chord V — an <u>imperfect cadence</u>. The <u>response</u> ends on note 1 or chord I — a <u>perfect cadence</u>. (See pp28-29 for more on cadences.)

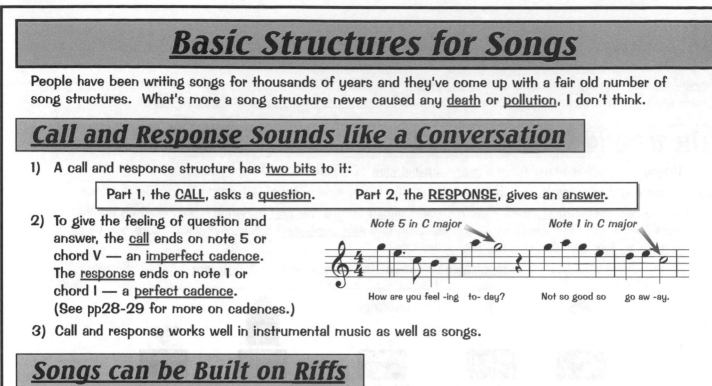

How are you feel -ing to- day?    Not so good so go aw -ay.

3) Call and response works well in instrumental music as well as songs.

## Songs can be Built on Riffs

1) A riff is a <u>short repeated tune</u>. If you put a few riffs together you can make a <u>whole song</u>.

2) A lot of <u>rock music</u> is riff-based. The <u>bass guitar</u> plays and repeats one short riff pattern. The <u>rhythm guitar</u> adds another harmonic riff and the drums add a rhythmic riff. The <u>lead guitar</u> adds a lead riff and the <u>singer</u> sings over all this. This creates <u>one section</u> of melody.

3) The riffs often <u>change</u> for the chorus.

## Ballads Tell Stories

1) The word <u>ballad</u> was originally used in the <u>15th century</u>. Back then it meant a long song with lots of verses that told a <u>story</u>. It's the type of thing that was sung by wandering <u>minstrels</u>.

2) If you hear people talking about ballads today they usually mean <u>pop</u> or <u>rock ballads</u> — songs that tell stories, often with a romantic or spooky <u>twist</u> that keeps people listening to the end.

3) Each verse has the <u>same</u> rhythm and tune.

## 12-Bar Blues Repeats a 12-Bar Structure

| BAR 1 | BAR 2 | BAR 3 | BAR 4 |
|-------|-------|-------|-------|
| Chord I | Chord I | Chord I | Chord I |

| BAR 5 | BAR 6 | BAR 7 | BAR 8 |
|-------|-------|-------|-------|
| Chord IV | Chord IV | Chord I | Chord I |

| BAR 9 | BAR 10 | BAR 11 | BAR 12 |
|-------|--------|--------|--------|
| Chord V | Chord IV | Chord I | Chord V |
|  |  |  | Chord I |

Last time

1) In 12-bar blues the main structure is <u>12 bars long</u>. (no kidding...)

2) The only chords are <u>I</u>, <u>IV</u> and <u>V</u>.

3) They're used in a <u>set pattern</u> through the 12 bars.

4) The 12-bar structure gets <u>repeated</u> through the song. To lead back into bar 1 you play <u>chord V</u> in bar 12 instead of chord I. Chord I is only actually played in bar 12 at the very end.

5) In the <u>tune</u> notes <u>3</u> and <u>7</u> are flattened — e.g. in G major, you play B♭ and F♮. These are the '<u>blue</u>' notes.

## 32-Bar Song Form is Very Very Simple

1) <u>32-bar</u> song form breaks down into <u>four 8-bar sections</u>.

2) Sections 1, 2 and 4 use the <u>main theme</u>. Section 3 uses a <u>contrasting theme</u>.

## Sing a song of sixpence — but I'd rather have twenty quid...

All these types of songs are just <u>basic</u> forms — there are <u>millions</u> of things you can do with each one to get different sounding songs. How else would record companies saturate the charts with <u>dross</u>...

# Basic Structures for Songs

This humdinger of a page goes through the different bits of a pop song.
By which I mean any song of the kind you'd hear on Radio 1, not Radio 3.

## The Main Sections are the Verse and Chorus

1) The verse always has the same tune, but the lyrics change in each verse.
2) The chorus has a different tune from the verse, usually quite a catchy one.
   The lyrics and tune of the chorus don't change.
3) The verse tells the story of the song. The chorus backs up the message of the story.
4) In a lot of songs, the verse and the chorus are both 8 bars long. This gives the song a balanced feel.
5) Most songs go verse, chorus, verse, chorus, etc. But there's no rule about this. You can use verses
   and choruses in any order you like, e.g. chorus, verse, verse, chorus, verse, chorus. It's up to you.

## The Middle 8 is an example of a Bridge

1) The middle 8 is an 8-bar section that's put into the middle of the song.
   It has new chords, new lyrics and a whole new feel.
2) The idea is to stop the audience from getting bored with the repeated
   verse and chorus. Just about every pop song has a middle 8.
3) A more general term for this 'break' in the song is a bridge, which can be as long or short as you like.
   Bridges are used to link different sections — verse and chorus, verse and verse, a slow bit and a fast bit...

## A Song Needs an Intro and a Coda

### INTRODUCTION

1) Introductions have two jobs. They grab the
   audience's attention and set the mood for
   the song.
2) If you're writing an intro it's a good idea to
   do it last, so you can use the best bit from
   the song to make people sit up and listen.

### CODA

1) The coda (or 'outro') is an ending that's
   different from the verse and the chorus.
2) You can use the coda to create a big
   finish, or just fade out.

## Instrumentals Let the Players Show Off

1) An instrumental section is one of those bits where the singer has a rest, and somebody
   else — maybe the lead guitar or keyboard — get to play their little hearts out.
2) They're no trouble to write (or improvise) because they use the same chords as the verse or chorus.
3) It sounds good to the audience because they already know the chords, so the
   instrumental sounds familiar even on the first hearing.

Put all the bits together and you end up with something like this:

INTRO | CHORUS | VERSE | CHORUS | VERSE | BRIDGE (middle 8) | CHORUS | BRIDGE | INSTRU-MENTAL | CHORUS | CODA (OUTRO)

## All together now...

When you break songs up into bits like this and give them formal names and everything it makes it all
sound really boring. Like maths or something. Rise above the boredom and learn the names — if you get
this type of song in your listening test you'll get loads more marks for using the proper terms.

# Sonata Form

Sonata form is <u>very tricky</u>, and given the choice I'd have left it out. But I'm afraid my hands are tied — if you want a top grade, you have to know this stuff. So — all you budding A and A* students, listen up...

## A Piece in Sonata Form has Three Main Sections

Exposition → Development → Recapitulation

Themes are "exposed" — heard for the first time.

Themes go through a number of interesting twists and turns.

Themes are "recapped" — played again.

## The Exposition has Two Themes

1) Having <u>two themes</u> lets you build up a <u>contrast</u> as you switch between them.

2) One theme could be <u>major</u> and the other <u>minor</u>. One could be <u>delicate</u> and the other <u>heavy</u>, or one could be <u>high</u> and the other <u>low</u>. It doesn't matter what the contrast is, so long as there <u>is</u> a contrast.

3) Some <u>Classical</u> sonatas have a slow-ish <u>introduction</u> before the main themes.

4) The exposition ends in a <u>different key</u> from the home key, and the whole section is marked to be <u>repeated</u>.

## The Development Keeps the Piece Interesting

In the middle section the themes get taken through lots of <u>variations</u>. You can vary them any way you like:

**SEQUENCING** page 44

**IMITATION** page 44

**PEDAL NOTE** (a note held on through different harmony changes)

**NEW HARMONIES** section 4

**AUGMENTATION AND DIMINUTION** page 45

**NEW RHYTHMS** pages 6 – 10

**INVERSION** page 45

*Have a look at the box on P. 35 for <u>more ideas</u> on varying your themes.*

Classical composers often <u>mixed</u> these techniques, e.g. sequencing an augmented version of one of the themes. Mixing and matching like this gives you loads of <u>possibilities</u> for your variations.

## The Recapitulation Pulls it All Together Again

1) If you're composing, this is the easy bit — the themes from the exposition are played <u>again</u>.

2) It's best not to do an <u>exact</u> repeat of the exposition. Make a few changes like adding <u>ornaments</u> or making the themes a bit <u>shorter</u>. This holds the listener's attention to the very <u>end</u>.

3) <u>Bridge sections</u> are used to link and modulate between two themes.

4) Composers usually add a coda to finish the piece off neatly. The traditional ending is a perfect cadence — but if it's your sonata, end it however you like.

5) For real <u>polish</u> add short link passages made up of <u>new material</u> between each of the three main sections. The final structure should look something like this:

| INTRODUCTION | EXPOSITION | DEVELOPMENT | RECAPITULATION | CODA |

## It's complicated — but that's no excuse for not learning it...

Sonata form is <u>frightfully sophisticated</u>, dah-ling. Get on top of it and you can feel really smug. Don't get muddled up between <u>sonata form</u> and <u>sonatas</u>. Sonatas <u>use</u> sonata form in the first movement, and sometimes the last one too — have a look at <u>page 39</u> opposite to find out more.

# Sonatas, Symphonies & Concertos

The examiners won't expect you to <u>write</u> anything this massive, but you <u>definitely</u> need to know all about them for the <u>listening</u> test. And for polite dinner party conversation when you're about 40. Maybe.

## Sonatas are for One or Two Instruments

1) Sonatas are mostly written for <u>one instrument</u>, but there are some sonatas for two instruments and a few for two <u>types</u> of instrument, each type playing different parts.

2) A sonata is usually in <u>three</u> or <u>four</u> sections (called <u>movements</u>), with <u>breaks</u> between them.

3) <u>At least one</u> of the movements is in sonata form (see P.38) — usually the first and sometimes the last.

## A Symphony is Played by a Full Orchestra

1) A symphony is a <u>massive</u> piece. They can last more than an hour and have real impact because of the full orchestra.

2) A symphony has the <u>same structure</u> as a sonata. They more often have <u>four movements</u> rather than three (and can have more than four).

3) Some symphonies have a <u>choir</u> as well as the orchestra.

> These chaps were all keen symphony writers...

| Haydn | Mozart | Beethoven | Schubert | Berlioz | Mendelssohn | Schumann | Brahms | Tchaikovsky | Mahler |
|-------|--------|-----------|----------|---------|-------------|----------|--------|-------------|--------|
| 1732 - 1809 | 1756 - 1791 | 1770 - 1827 | 1797 - 1828 | 1803 - 1869 | 1809 - 1847 | 1810 - 1856 | 1833 - 1897 | 1840 - 1893 | 1860 - 1911 |

## A Concerto is for a Solo Instrument and an Orchestra

1) The <u>soloist</u> has most of the <u>tune</u>, and gets to really show off how brilliant they are.

2) The <u>orchestra</u> has the tune some of the time too though. Their part's a bit <u>more</u> than an **accompaniment**.

3) There are usually <u>three movements</u> — quick, slow and quick.

## There are Standard Forms for 4-Movement Compositions

Sonatas, symphonies and concertos all follow the same <u>basic plan</u>. These are the traditional forms used by composers for each of the movements.

| | | |
|---|---|---|
| **FIRST MOVEMENT** | sonata form | brisk and purposeful |
| **SECOND MOVEMENT** | ternary or variation form | slower and songlike |
| **THIRD MOVEMENT** | minuet or scherzo | fairly fast and dance-like |
| **FOURTH MOVEMENT** | rondo, variation or sonata form | fast and cheerful |

*This one's <u>left out</u> of <u>sonatas in three movements</u> and <u>concertos</u>.*

## Just one concerto, play it for me...

There are <u>thousands</u> of sonatas, symphonies and concertos. Western composers have been churning them out since the sixteenth century. In some ways they're quite similar, so learn this page really carefully, and make sure you know the differences — <u>how many movements</u> and <u>who</u> plays them.

# Opera & Oratorio

Opera and oratorio are forms you'll need to know for <u>listening</u>. If you write a whole oratorio for your composition, the examiners will be so impressed they'll probably fall down in a <u>faint</u>. Very undignified.

## Operas are like Plays set to Music

1) The <u>main characters</u> are played by <u>solo singers</u>.
2) The main characters are supported by a <u>chorus</u> and an <u>orchestra</u>.
3) The story is <u>acted out</u> — usually with <u>lavish sets</u>, <u>costumes</u> and <u>special effects</u>.
4) In some operas <u>every single word</u> is sung — in others there's a bit of <u>talking</u> from time to time.
5) Some operas have really serious, <u>tragic</u> themes. Others are more light-hearted and <u>comic</u>. These are the names for the main types.
6) The words of an opera are called the '<u>libretto</u>'. This is often written by a 'librettist' working alongside the composer.

| Grand opera | set entirely to music / serious |
|---|---|
| Opéra comique | some spoken dialogue |
| Opera buffa | comic opera |
| Opera seria | formal, serious opera |

## In Opera there are Three Types of Singing

### ARIA
1) An <u>aria</u> is a <u>solo</u> vocal piece, backed by the orchestra.
2) Arias are used to go into the <u>emotions</u> of the main characters.
3) The arias have the <u>memorable</u>, <u>exciting tunes</u>. They're <u>challenging</u> for the performers and let them show their vocal <u>tone</u> and <u>agility</u>.

### RECITATIVE
1) <u>Recitative</u> is a half-spoken, half-singing style used for some <u>conversations</u>.
2) <u>Recitativo secco</u> is recitative that's <u>unaccompanied</u> or backed by <u>simple chords</u>.
3) <u>Recitativo stromentato</u> or <u>accompagnato</u> is recitative with orchestral backing. The accompaniment's used to increase the <u>dramatic tension</u> of the words.

### CHORUS
A bit where the <u>whole chorus</u> sings together.

## Oratorio is the Religious Version of Opera

1) An oratorio has <u>arias</u>, <u>recitatives</u> and <u>choruses</u> just like an opera.
2) Oratorios usually have a <u>religious theme</u>. They're based on <u>traditional stories</u>, sometimes from the Bible.
3) Oratorios don't usually have scenery, costumes or action — they're <u>not acted out</u>.
4) Oratorios were written mainly for <u>concert</u> or <u>church</u> performance.

| Composer | Lived | Famous Oratorio |
|---|---|---|
| Carissimi | 1605 - 1674 | Jephte |
| Handel | 1685 - 1759 | Messiah |
| Haydn | 1732 - 1809 | The Creation |
| Berlioz | 1803 - 1869 | L'Enfance du Christ |
| Mendelssohn | 1809 - 1847 | Elijah |
| Elgar | 1857 - 1934 | The Dream of Gerontius |
| Walton | 1902 - 1983 | Belshazzar's Feast |

## The show ain't over till the fat lady sings...

Actually, nowadays, most opera singers are pretty skinny. The women are, anyway. In olden times (up until about twenty years ago) they used to think they'd lose their singing powers if they lost weight. They also used to swallow live worms to make their voices <u>smooth</u> and <u>lovely</u>. Or so I've been told.

# Smaller Vocal Pieces

These songs are shorter than operas and the like, but you still need to know their <u>forms</u>...

## Lots of Music was Written to be Sung in Church

### CANTATA

Some things in a <u>cantata</u> are similar to <u>oratorio</u>. The performers are <u>solo singers</u>, a <u>chorus</u> and an <u>orchestra</u>. There's <u>no scenery</u> and <u>no acting</u> and they were written to be performed in a <u>church</u> or <u>concert hall</u>.

The <u>difference</u> is that the <u>words</u> are taken from books or poems — they're not specially written. Most cantatas have a religious theme — but <u>not all</u> of them.

### CHORALE

<u>Chorales</u> are hymns. They have <u>simple language</u> and a melody that's <u>easy to sing</u>. J.S. Bach wrote stacks of them. Here's a bit from a chorale he put in *St. Matthew's Passion.*

O Lord, who dares to smite Thee?

### MOTET & ANTHEM

A <u>motet</u>'s a short piece written to be performed by the <u>choir</u> in church. They're written for <u>Roman Catholic</u> churches and the words are often in <u>Latin</u>. Motets are <u>polyphonic</u> — see P.31.

An <u>anthem</u> is very similar to a motet except they're written for <u>Protestant</u> churches, so the words aren't in Latin.

### MASS

The <u>mass</u> is the name of a Roman Catholic church service — these parts of the mass are sung by the choir, or the choir and soloists:

Musical settings of the Mass were originally written to be <u>used in church</u>, but nowadays they're played in concerts, too. The text is usually in <u>Latin</u>.

- Kyrie — *Lord have mercy...*
- Gloria — *Glory be to God on high...*
- Credo — *I believe in one God...*
- Sanctus — *Holy, holy, holy...*
- Benedictus — *Blessed is He...*
- Agnus Dei — *O Lamb of God...*

*(Some of them are quite long, so I've only given you the starting bits.)*

## Madrigals and Lieder are non-Religious

Most madrigals were written in the <u>1500s</u> and <u>1600s</u>. They're about love or the countryside — or both. Most have <u>no accompaniment</u> and each person sings a <u>different part</u>. Madrigals often use <u>imitation</u> (see P.44).

Now is the month of May-ing, When mer-ry lads are play-ing; Fa la la la la la la la la, Fa la la la la la la.

A <u>lied</u>'s a <u>song</u> for <u>one singer</u> and a <u>piano</u>. Both parts are equally important. The words really matter too — they're usually based on <u>poems</u>. Lieder were massively popular in the <u>German Romantic</u> period (late 18th to early 19th century).

To wan-der is the mil-ler's joy, to wan -der

*From The Wandering Miller by Schubert. He wrote over 600 top quality lieder.*

## They don't seem to have mentioned karaoke...

'<u>Lied</u>' is the German word for '<u>song</u>'. It's pronounced **LEED**. If you're talking about <u>more than one</u> lied you say <u>lieder</u> (not 'lieds'). Here endeth the German lesson.

# Revision Summary

This section's been a living nightmare of technical terms, tricky ideas and generally complex stuff that needs remembering. But lookee here... what light through yonder cloud of revision gloom breaks? It is the revision summary questions, and they will save your skin. When you feel like you've got to grips with the section, have a go at these. When you can answer them all without looking back, you really _have_ got to grips with the section...

1)   Give an example of contrasting sections in a song.

2)   How many sections are there in a piece in:
     a) binary form      b) ternary form?

3)   Is a piece that's organised "A, B, A1" in binary form, or ternary form?

4)   What does _rondo_ mean?

5)   How many sections are there in a piece in rondo form?

6)   When you use letters to stand for the names of the different sections, does "B" stand for:
     a) main theme      b)  a contrasting theme?

7)   Is theme and variation form one continuous piece of music, or are there gaps between sections?

8)   Write down six different ways you can vary the main theme in a theme and variation piece.

9)   What are the main differences between theme and variation form and ground bass form?

10)  In call and response, what type of cadences end the "call" and the "response"?

11)  What's a riff?

12)  What do the lyrics do in a ballad?

13)  What chords do you get in 12-bar blues?

14)  How do you make a 12-bar blues song longer than 12 bars?

15)  Draw a diagram of a song in 32-bar song form, using a labelled box for each section.

16)  Write true or false for each of these.  In a pop song:
     a)  the verse has the same words every time
     b)  the chorus tells the story
     c)  the middle 8 sounds much the same as the verse and chorus
     d)  when James Brown said "Take it to the bridge" he meant the Hammersmith Flyover
     e)  the intro is always quiet

17)  What order do these sections come in, in sonata form?  Development, Exposition, Recapitulation.

18)  Write down at least five ways of varying the themes in a sonata.

19)  Where would you use an introduction, coda, links and bridges in sonata form?

20)  Write down how many performers, how many movements and what the movements are like for each
     of these: a) sonata      b)  symphony      c)  concerto.

21)  What are the words of an opera called?

22)  What are the three main singing styles in an opera?

23)  Write down three differences and three similarities between opera and oratorio.

24)  What's the difference between a motet and an anthem?

25)  Write down the six main parts of a mass.

26)  How many performers perform a lied?

27)  When were madrigals written?

# Coming Up with a Composition

Using all the bits and bobs from the last five sections, you should be able to <u>write a piece of your own</u> now.
If you're not sure where to start, try following these instructions for a <u>composition</u> in <u>ternary form</u>.

## 1) Start by Working Out an 8-Bar Rhythm

1) First compose a <u>4-bar rhythm</u>. End it in a longish note, e.g. crotchet or minim. This is the <u>question phrase</u>.

2) Compose another <u>4-bar rhythm</u>. This is the <u>answering phrase</u>. End on a long note and <u>repeat</u> some of the rhythm patterns from the question in the answer.

Phrase 1 "question"  Phrase 2 "answer"

3) Don't worry about the <u>pitch</u> of the notes, just sort out the <u>rhythm</u>.

## 2) Turn the Rhythm into a Melody

1) Choose a <u>scale</u> to get your notes from. <u>C major</u>'s dead easy — it only uses the <u>white notes</u> on the keyboard — C, D, E, F, G, A, B and C.

2) Make the <u>first</u> and <u>last</u> note of your melody the same as <u>note 1</u> of your scale. In C major it's <u>C</u>.

3) Make the <u>last note</u> of <u>bar 4</u> the same as <u>note 5</u> of your scale. Note 5 of C major is <u>G</u>.

Phrase 1 "question"  Phrase 2 "answer"

Note 1  Note 5  Note 1
C  G  C

4) Give the rest of the notes letter names <u>from your scale</u>. The melody will sound better if it moves up and down in <u>steps</u> or with just <u>small leaps</u>.

*It's fine to use the same note several times.*

## 3) Write Another 8 Bars to get a Piece in Ternary Form

1) A piece in <u>ternary form</u> (P. 34) has <u>three sections</u>, two the same, and one different — ABA.

2) You've <u>already got</u> Section A — it's your 8-bar composition. For <u>Section B</u> compose <u>another 8 bars</u> the same way you did for Section A.

3) Section B needs to <u>contrast</u> with Section A. An easy-ish way is to use a <u>different scale</u>, related to the one you used for Section A (see P. 16 and P. 30). E.g. if Section A's in <u>C major</u> you could put Section B in the <u>dominant key — G major</u>, or the <u>relative minor — A minor</u>.

4) Play <u>ABA</u> and you've got a complete piece in ternary form.

## 4) Add a Harmony

1) If you want to add a <u>harmony</u> have a look at <u>Section 4</u> on chords.

2) It works well to <u>include</u> the note you're harmonising with in the chord.

3) Always use <u>cadences</u> (P.28 and P.29) to finish off phrases.

## Compose yourself — this isn't that bad...

<u>Checking</u>'s never a bad idea. Check that the <u>beats</u> in every bar add up to the number of beats in the key signature. Check that you haven't got any notes from random <u>keys</u>. The best thing to do is <u>play it</u>.

# Ways to Vary a Composition

There are lots of ways composers make their <u>rhythms</u> and <u>melodies</u> more interesting. Even if you don't want to use these yourself, learn what they're called, in case they come up in your listening test.

## Sandwich Contrasting Melodies

1) If a simple <u>phrase</u> works well you can <u>repeat it</u>.

2) For variety, put a <u>contrasting</u> phrase between the repeated bits.

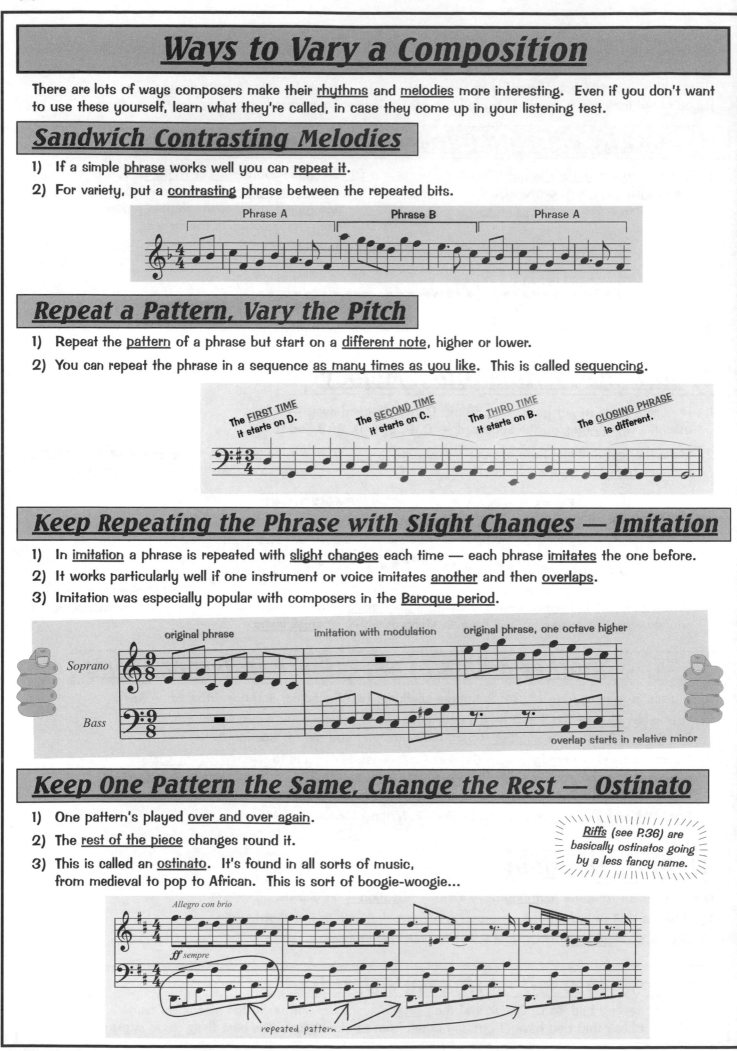

Phrase A          Phrase B          Phrase A

## Repeat a Pattern, Vary the Pitch

1) Repeat the <u>pattern</u> of a phrase but start on a <u>different note</u>, higher or lower.

2) You can repeat the phrase in a sequence <u>as many times as you like</u>. This is called <u>sequencing</u>.

The <u>FIRST TIME</u> it starts on D.   The <u>SECOND TIME</u> it starts on C.   The <u>THIRD TIME</u> it starts on B.   The <u>CLOSING PHRASE</u> is different.

## Keep Repeating the Phrase with Slight Changes — Imitation

1) In <u>imitation</u> a phrase is repeated with <u>slight changes</u> each time — each phrase <u>imitates</u> the one before.

2) It works particularly well if one instrument or voice imitates <u>another</u> and then <u>overlaps</u>.

3) Imitation was especially popular with composers in the <u>Baroque period</u>.

original phrase          imitation with modulation          original phrase, one octave higher

Soprano

Bass

overlap starts in relative minor

## Keep One Pattern the Same, Change the Rest — Ostinato

1) One pattern's played <u>over and over again</u>.

2) The <u>rest of the piece</u> changes round it.

3) This is called an <u>ostinato</u>. It's found in all sorts of music, from medieval to pop to African. This is sort of boogie-woogie...

> *Riffs* (see P.36) are basically ostinatos going by a less fancy name.

Allegro con brio

ff sempre

repeated pattern

# Ways to Vary a Composition

## Change the Rhythm

You can get a new version of the melody by <u>lengthening</u> or <u>shortening</u> the notes.

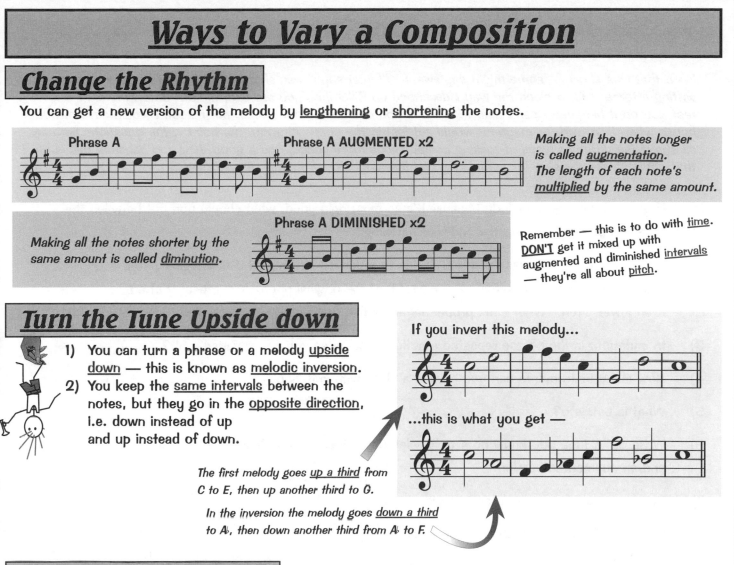

*Making all the notes longer is called <u>augmentation</u>. The length of each note's <u>multiplied</u> by the same amount.*

*Making all the notes shorter by the same amount is called <u>diminution</u>.*

Remember — this is to do with <u>time</u>. <u>DON'T</u> get it mixed up with augmented and diminished <u>intervals</u> — they're all about <u>pitch</u>.

## Turn the Tune Upside down

1) You can turn a phrase or a melody <u>upside down</u> — this is known as <u>melodic inversion</u>.
2) You keep the <u>same intervals</u> between the notes, but they go in the <u>opposite direction</u>, i.e. down instead of up and up instead of down.

*If you invert this melody...*

*...this is what you get —*

*The first melody goes <u>up a third</u> from C to E, then up another third to G.*

*In the inversion the melody goes <u>down a third</u> to A♭, then down another third from A♭ to F.*

## Jazz Up the Rhythms

1) Normally the <u>main accent</u> (emphasis) in a bar comes on the <u>first beat</u>. The accent can be shifted to another beat to give an <u>offbeat</u> sound. This is called <u>syncopation</u>, and you hear a lot of these rhythms in <u>jazz</u>.

Here's that old favourite, 'Twinkle, Twinkle' with some accents on the offbeat:

2) Another way to make the rhythm syncopated is to shift <u>all</u> the accents across by the <u>same</u> amount, like so:

3) If the beats are divided up in <u>different ways</u> and the accents fall in <u>different places</u> in the different parts, it's called <u>cross-rhythm</u>.

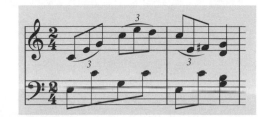

## So many variations — so little time...

Composing's a bit like ordering <u>pizza</u>. Well, actually it's not, but at least I've got your attention. Don't try and use all these variations at once — if you do you could change your tune so much that it's unrecognisable. Just try using one or two effects at a time. And hold the <u>anchovies</u>.

# Revision Summary

*Well, that was short — some might say sweet. I'll just say it was short. If you want to have a go at writing a ternary form piece the way I described on P.43 then you are GREAT. But unfortunately I can't test you on it because I can't hear it. I mean you could send me a tape, but maybe I would have moved house when it arrived, or maybe it would get lost in the post. Anyway, the point is the questions here are all about the different ways of making compositions more varied, and a good thing too because this is stuff that could save your skin for composing <u>and</u> listening. Read on and answer away.*

1) If you're repeating a melody because it's so amazingly good, what should you put between the repeated phrases to keep the audience listening?

2) You've got a lovely phrase and you decide to reuse it. You repeat it at a higher pitch. You repeat it at a lower pitch. You repeat it at the original pitch. You repeat it at an even lower pitch. What's the proper name for this technique?

3) In imitation, is the phrase repeated exactly the same each time, or varied a bit?

4) How many instruments can you have in a piece with imitation?

5) What is ostinato?

6) Write out a tune you know on a treble clef stave, then write a diminished version and an augmented version.

7) Describe what is meant by an inversion.

8) Write a definition for each of these ways of varying the beat:
   a) offbeat
   b) syncopated
   c) cross-rhythm

*Section Six — Composing*

# Brass Instruments

You probably know quite a bit about <u>your</u> instrument. It helps when you're playing, or singing, with other people to know a bit about their instruments too, so you can understand what they're up to. <u>Brass</u> first.

## Brass Instruments are All Made of Metal   *(though not always brass)*

1) Brass instruments are <u>horns</u>, <u>trumpets</u>, <u>cornets</u>, <u>trombones</u> and <u>tubas</u>.

2) They're all basically a length of <u>hollow</u>, <u>metal tubing</u> with a <u>mouthpiece</u> (the bit you blow into) at one end and a <u>funnel shape</u> (the <u>bell</u>) at the other.

3) The different <u>shapes</u> and <u>sizes</u> of these parts gives each brass instrument a different tone and character.

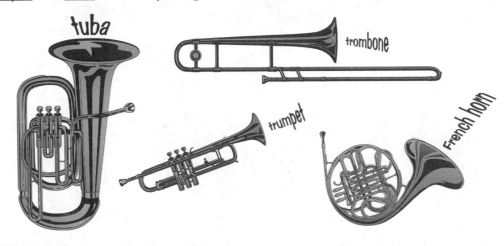

## You Get a Noise by 'Buzzing' your Lips

1) To <u>make a sound</u> on a brass instrument, you have to make the air <u>vibrate</u> down the tube.

2) You do it by '<u>buzzing</u>' your lips into the <u>mouthpiece</u>. You <u>squeeze</u> your lips together, then <u>blow</u> through a tiny gap so you get a <u>buzzing noise</u>. You know you've got it right when it really <u>tickles</u>.

3) You have to squeeze your lips together <u>tighter</u> to get <u>higher notes</u>.

## Brass Instruments Use Slides and Valves to Change Pitch

1) Squeezing your lips only gets a <u>limited range</u> of notes. To get a decent range brass instruments use <u>slides</u> (like on a trombone) or <u>valves</u> (like on a trumpet).

2) The <u>slide</u> on a trombone is the <u>U-shaped tube</u> that moves in and out of the main tube. Moving it <u>out</u> makes the tube <u>longer</u> so you get a <u>lower</u> note. Moving it in makes the tube <u>shorter</u> so you get a <u>higher</u> note.

3) <u>Horns</u>, <u>trumpets</u> and <u>cornets</u> use three buttons connected to <u>valves</u>. The valves <u>open</u> and <u>close</u> different sections of the tube to make it <u>longer</u> or <u>shorter</u>. Pressing down the buttons in <u>different combinations</u> gives you all the notes you need.

## Brass Players use Mutes to Change the Tone

1) A <u>mute</u> is a kind of <u>bung</u> that's put in the <u>bell</u> of a brass instrument. It's used to make the instrument play more <u>quietly</u> and change the <u>tone</u>. You wouldn't usually use one all the way through a piece — just for a <u>short section</u>.

2) <u>Different shapes</u> and <u>sizes</u> of mute change the tone in different ways, e.g. the <u>wowwow</u> mute gives the instrument a wowwow sound. *I bet you never would have guessed...*

## Brassed off — how could you be, revising's so much fun...

If you get brass in a listening test and need to say what instrument it is, remember the <u>bigger</u> instruments generally play <u>lower</u> notes and <u>smaller</u> instruments play <u>higher</u> notes. Tuba's sound like they're farting. Sorry if that's a bit immature of me, but it's true. *Oom parp-parp, oom parp-parp...*

# Woodwind

People sometimes get woodwind and brass muddled up. If you're one of them <u>learn the difference</u>.

## Woodwind Instruments used to be Made of Wood

<u>Woodwind</u> instruments got their name because they all use <u>air</u> — wind — to make a sound and once upon a time were all made of <u>wood</u>. Nowadays some are still made of <u>wood</u>. Others are made of <u>plastic</u> or <u>silver</u>. These are the main ones:

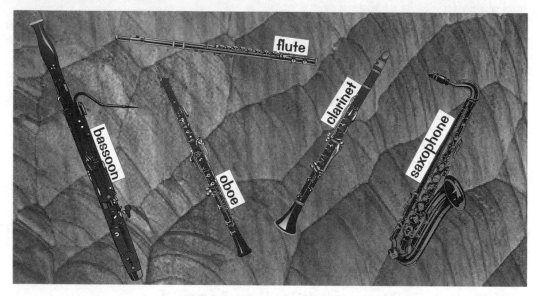

## Woodwind Instruments Make Sound in Different Ways

To get a <u>sound</u> from a <u>wind</u> instrument, you have to make the <u>air</u> in its tube <u>vibrate</u>. There are <u>three different ways</u> woodwind instruments do this:

1) <u>EDGE-TONE INSTRUMENTS</u> — <u>flutes</u> and <u>piccolos</u>. Air's blown across an <u>oval-shaped hole</u>. The <u>edge</u> of the hole <u>splits</u> the air. This makes it <u>vibrate</u> down the instrument and make the sound.

 2) <u>SINGLE-REED INSTRUMENTS</u> — <u>clarinets</u> and <u>saxophones</u>. Air is blown down a mouthpiece which has a reed — a thin slice of wood/reed/plastic — clamped to it. The reed <u>vibrates</u>, making the air in the instrument vibrate, and creating the sound.

3) <u>DOUBLE-REED INSTRUMENTS</u> — <u>oboes</u> and <u>bassoons</u>. The air passes between two reeds, tightly bound together and squeezed between the lips. The reeds vibrate and you get a sound.

## Different Notes are made by Opening and Closing Holes

1) Wind instruments are covered in <u>keys</u>, <u>springs</u> and <u>levers</u>. These operate little <u>pads</u> that <u>close</u> and <u>open</u> holes down the instrument.

2) Opening and closing holes effectively makes the instrument longer or shorter. The <u>shorter</u> the tube, the <u>higher</u> the note. The <u>longer</u> the tube, the <u>lower</u> the note.

### I can't see the woodwind for the clarinets...

Flutes and saxophones are made of metal but they're still <u>wood</u>wind instruments. If you're still confused remember that woodwind instruments sound more <u>breathy</u>, and brass instruments sound well... farty...

# Orchestral Strings

Orchestral strings are the <u>heart</u> of the orchestra — or so string players would have you believe.

## The Double Bass, Cello, Viola and Violin are Very Alike

These are all <u>made</u> and played in a <u>similar way</u>.
The main differences are the <u>size</u> and <u>pitch</u>.

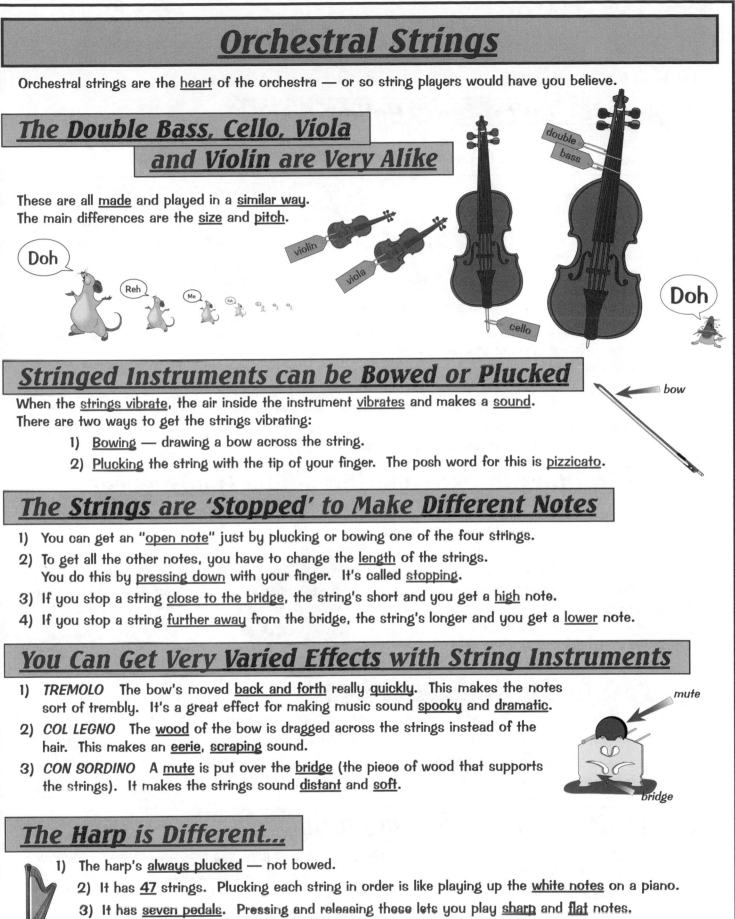

## Stringed Instruments can be Bowed or Plucked

When the <u>strings vibrate</u>, the air inside the instrument <u>vibrates</u> and makes a <u>sound</u>.
There are two ways to get the strings vibrating:

1) <u>Bowing</u> — drawing a bow across the string.

2) <u>Plucking</u> the string with the tip of your finger. The posh word for this is <u>pizzicato</u>.

## The Strings are 'Stopped' to Make Different Notes

1) You can get an "<u>open note</u>" just by plucking or bowing one of the four strings.

2) To get all the other notes, you have to change the <u>length</u> of the strings.
You do this by <u>pressing down</u> with your finger. It's called <u>stopping</u>.

3) If you stop a string <u>close to the bridge</u>, the string's short and you get a <u>high</u> note.

4) If you stop a string <u>further away</u> from the bridge, the string's longer and you get a <u>lower</u> note.

## You Can Get Very Varied Effects with String Instruments

1) *TREMOLO*  The bow's moved <u>back and forth</u> really <u>quickly</u>. This makes the notes
sort of trembly. It's a great effect for making music sound <u>spooky</u> and <u>dramatic</u>.

2) *COL LEGNO*  The <u>wood</u> of the bow is dragged across the strings instead of the
hair. This makes an <u>eerie</u>, <u>scraping</u> sound.

3) *CON SORDINO*  A <u>mute</u> is put over the <u>bridge</u> (the piece of wood that supports
the strings). It makes the strings sound <u>distant</u> and <u>soft</u>.

## The Harp is Different...

1) The harp's <u>always plucked</u> — not bowed.

2) It has <u>47</u> strings. Plucking each string in order is like playing up the <u>white notes</u> on a piano.

3) It has <u>seven pedals</u>. Pressing and releasing these lets you play <u>sharp</u> and <u>flat</u> notes.

4) You can play <u>one</u> note at a time, or play <u>chords</u> by plucking a few strings together.

## Violinists are always in tears — too highly strung...

Violins are played in folk music, country, jazz and naff pop songs, and a jazz band would only be half there
if it didn't have a double bass. So these instruments are <u>sometimes</u> "orchestral" but not always.

# Guitars

Guitars are bloomin' <u>everywhere</u>. So it's best to know a bit about how they work.

## An Acoustic Guitar has a Hollow Body

The <u>acoustic guitar</u> makes a sound the same way as the orchestral strings — by vibrating air in its belly. Slightly different types are used by pop, folk and classical guitarists, but the <u>basic design</u> is similar.

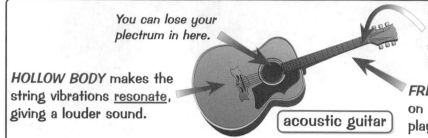

*You can lose your plectrum in here.*

**STRINGS** tuned to the notes E(low)-A-D-G-B-E(high). Low E is the string nearest to you as you're playing. Played with <u>fingers</u> or a <u>plectrum</u>.

*HOLLOW BODY* makes the string vibrations <u>resonate</u>, giving a louder sound.

acoustic guitar

**FRETS** (the little metal strips on the fingerboard) help the player find the <u>correct finger position</u> for different notes.

There are three different kinds of acoustic guitar:

1) The <u>classical</u> or <u>Spanish</u> guitar — has nylon strings (the thickest three are covered in fine wire) and a thick neck.

2) The <u>acoustic guitar</u> — has <u>steel strings</u> and is used mainly in pop and folk music. Its neck is <u>thinner</u> and is <u>strengthened</u> with a metal bar — this supports the higher tension created by the steel strings.

3) The <u>12-stringed guitar</u> — often used in folk music. There are two of each string — this gives a 'thicker' sound which works well for accompanying singing.

## Electric Guitars Use an Amplifier and a Loudspeaker

1) An electric guitar has <u>six strings</u>, just like an acoustic guitar, and is <u>played</u> in a similar way.

2) The main difference is that an electric guitar has a <u>solid body</u>. The sound's made louder <u>electrically</u>, using an <u>amplifier</u> and a <u>loudspeaker</u>.

3) A <u>combo</u> — short for combination — is an <u>amplifier</u> and <u>loudspeaker</u> '<u>all in one</u>'.

electric guitar

*You can't lose your plectrum in here.*

*A <u>semi-acoustic</u> electric guitar has a hollow body to <u>naturally</u> amplify sounds <u>and</u> all the right fiddly knobs to be plugged in and played <u>electrically</u>.*

## The Bass Guitar has Four Strings

1) The bass guitar works just the same way as the guitar except it has <u>four strings</u>, not six.

2) They're tuned to the notes <u>E-A-D-G</u> (from lowest note to highest).

3) It's <u>lower pitched</u> than other guitars because it has <u>thicker and longer</u> strings.

4) Most bass guitars have frets, but there are some — imaginatively named <u>fretless basses</u> — that don't.

*Like ordinary guitars, you can get electric or acoustic basses.*

## Guitar Strings are Picked or Strummed

1) Plucking <u>one string</u> at a time is called <u>picking</u>. <u>Classical</u> and <u>lead guitarists</u> pick the notes of a <u>melody</u>. <u>Bass</u> guitarists <u>always</u> pick out the individual notes of a bass line. They <u>never strum</u>.

2) Playing <u>two or more</u> strings at a time is called <u>strumming</u>. It's how you play <u>chords</u>. <u>Pop</u> and <u>folk</u> <u>guitarists</u> tend to play <u>accompaniments</u> rather than tunes, so they do more strumming than picking.

3) A <u>plectrum</u> is a small, flat piece of plastic that guitarists can use to pluck or strum with — it's kind of like having an extra long fingernail.

## Who says the air guitar's not a proper instrument...

Learn those different <u>playing techniques</u> and if you hear them in the exam, use the proper words — <u>picking</u> and <u>strumming</u> — to describe them. The examiners'll think all their Christmases have come at once.

# Keyboard Instruments

The actual <u>keyboard</u> looks much the same on most keyboard instruments, but the wires and mysterious levers <u>inside</u> vary quite a bit, and that means the <u>sounds</u> they make vary too.

## Harpsichords, Virginals and Clavichords Came First

1) Harpsichords were invented long before pianos. They're still played today but they were <u>most popular</u> in the <u>Baroque</u> and <u>early classical</u> periods.

2) Harpsichords have quite a <u>tinny</u>, <u>string</u> sound. When you press a key a string inside is <u>plucked</u> by a lever. You can't vary the <u>strength</u> of the pluck, so you <u>can't</u> vary the <u>dynamics</u>.

3) A <u>virginal</u> is a miniature table-top version of a harpsichord. In the sixteenth century virginals were really popular in England.

4) The <u>clavichord</u> is another early keyboard instrument. Clavichords are small and have a <u>soft</u> sound. The strings are <u>struck</u> with hammers, not plucked, so you can vary the dynamics a little bit.

*This fella's a harpsichord.*

## The Most Popular Keyboard Instrument Now is the Piano

1) The piano was invented around <u>1700</u>. The <u>technology</u> is <u>more sophisticated</u> than it was in earlier keyboard instruments. When a key's pressed, a hammer hits the strings. The <u>harder</u> you hit the key, the <u>harder</u> the hammer hits the strings and the <u>louder</u> the note — so there's a big range of <u>dynamics</u>.

2) Pianos have a wide range of <u>notes</u> — up to <u>seven and a half octaves</u>.

3) Pianos have <u>pedals</u> that let you change the sound in different ways.

The <u>soft</u> pedal on the left <u>mutes</u> the strings, making a softer sound.

The <u>sustain</u> pedal on the right <u>lifts</u> all the <u>dampers</u>. This lets the sound <u>ring on</u> until you release the pedal.

<u>Grand pianos</u> have a <u>middle pedal</u> too. This lets the player <u>choose</u> which notes to sustain.

## Traditional Organs Use Pumped Air to Make Sound

1) The traditional organ — the <u>massive instrument</u> with hundreds of metal pipes that you see at the back of churches and concert halls — is one of the most <u>complicated</u> instruments ever designed.

2) Sound's made by <u>blowing air</u> through sets of pipes called <u>ranks</u>. The air's pumped in by <u>hand</u>, <u>foot</u> or, on more recent organs, using <u>electric pumps</u>.

3) The pipes are controlled by <u>keyboards</u>, called <u>manuals</u>, and lots of <u>pedals</u> which make a keyboard for the player's feet.

4) <u>Pressing</u> a key or pedal lets air pass through one of the pipes and play a note. <u>Longer</u> pipes make <u>lower</u> notes. <u>Shorter</u> pipes make <u>higher</u> notes.

5) Organs can play <u>different types of sound</u> by using differently designed pipes. Buttons called <u>stops</u> are used to select the different pipes. One stop might select pipes that make a <u>trumpet</u> sound, another might select a <u>flute</u> sound...

6) Modern <u>electronic organs</u> don't have pipes. Sound is produced by <u>electricity</u> instead. These organs are much <u>smaller</u> and <u>cheaper</u> to build.

## No back-pedalling — get keyed in and learn it all...

The sound harpsichords make compared with pianos is <u>jangly</u>. Not a very technical word, but it'll do. You can easily identify an organ sound, though you might not know whether it's a "real" one or an electronic one. Another name for those big organs with all the pipes is the <u>King of Instruments</u>. Isn't that nice.

# Percussion

A percussion instrument is anything you have to <u>hit</u> or <u>shake</u> to get a sound out of it. There are <u>two types</u>: the ones that can play tunes are called <u>tuned percussion</u>, ones you just hit are <u>untuned</u>.

## Tuned Percussion can Play Different Notes

**XYLOPHONES** have <u>wooden</u> bars. The sound is '<u>woody</u>'.

**GLOCKENSPIEL** — Looks a bit like a xylophone but the bars are made of <u>metal</u>. Sounds <u>tinkly</u> and <u>bell-like</u>.

**CELESTA** — a bit like a glockenspiel except that you use a <u>keyboard</u> instead of whacking with a hammer.

**TUBULAR BELLS** — Each of the <u>hollow steel tubes</u> plays a different note. Sounds a bit like <u>church bells</u>.

**TIMPANI** — also called <u>kettledrums</u>. The handles on the side or the foot pedals can be used to tighten or relax the skin, giving <u>different notes</u>.

**VIBRAPHONE** — This is like a <u>giant glockenspiel</u>. There are long tubes called <u>resonators</u> below the bars to make the notes <u>louder</u> and <u>richer</u>. <u>Electric fans</u> make the notes <u>pulsate</u> giving a warm and gentle sound.

## There are Hundreds of Untuned Percussion Instruments

<u>Untuned percussion</u> includes any instrument that'll <u>make a noise</u> — but <u>can't</u> play a tune. These are the instruments that are used for <u>pure rhythm</u>. It's pretty much <u>impossible</u> to learn <u>every</u> untuned percussion instrument, but try and remember the names of these...

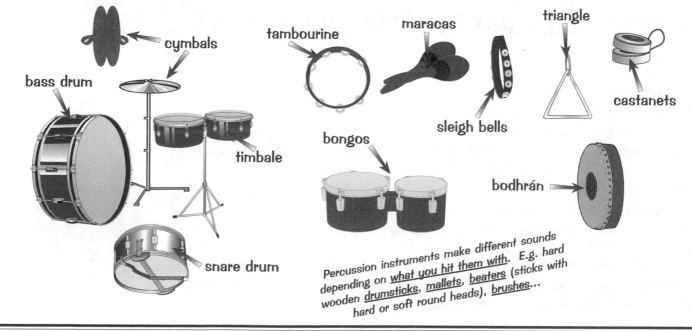

cymbals, bass drum, tambourine, maracas, triangle, castanets, sleigh bells, timbale, bongos, bodhrán, snare drum

Percussion instruments make different sounds depending on <u>what you hit them with</u>. E.g. hard wooden <u>drumsticks</u>, <u>mallets</u>, <u>beaters</u> (sticks with hard or soft round heads), <u>brushes</u>...

## Hit me baby one more time...

In a band the point of having a drummer is to add a healthy dollop of <u>rhythm</u>, which makes the song sound like it's going somewhere and keeps everyone in time. In an orchestra the percussion's more there to add <u>special effects</u> — like thundery drum rolls on the timpani or huge clashes of the cymbals.

# The Voice

Music being music, there are special names for male and female <u>voices</u> and <u>groups</u> of voices.

## Female Singers are Soprano, Alto or Mezzo-Soprano

1) A <u>high</u> female voice is called a <u>soprano</u>. The main female parts in operas are sung by sopranos.

2) A <u>lower</u> female voice is called an <u>alto</u> — short for <u>contralto</u>.

3) <u>Mezzo-sopranos</u> sing in the <u>top</u> part of the <u>alto</u> range and the <u>bottom</u> part of the <u>soprano</u> range.

## Male Voices are Tenor or Bass

1) <u>Higher</u> male voices are called <u>tenors</u>.

2) <u>Low</u> male voices are called <u>basses</u> (it's pronounced "bases").

3) <u>Baritones</u> sing the <u>top</u> part of the <u>bass</u> range and the <u>bottom</u> part of the <u>tenor</u> range.

4) Men with an <u>alto</u> voice are simply called <u>male altos</u>.

5) Some men can push their voices <u>higher</u> to sing some of the same notes as a soprano. This is called <u>falsetto</u> singing.

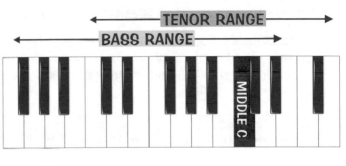

## Children's Voices are either Treble or Alto

1) A <u>high child's</u> voice in the <u>same range</u> as a <u>soprano</u> is called a <u>treble</u>.

2) A <u>low child's</u> voice is called an <u>alto</u>. They sing in exactly the <u>same range</u> as an adult alto.

3) Girls' voices don't change much as they get older. Boys' voices <u>drop</u> to a <u>lower range</u> when they hit puberty.

## When Several Voices Sing Each Part it's a Choir

1) A <u>choir</u> is a group of singers. Each part is performed by <u>more than one</u> singer.

2) A <u>mixed voice choir</u> has sopranos, altos, tenors and basses. These are called <u>S.A.T.B.</u> for short.

3) An <u>all-male choir</u> has trebles, altos, tenors and basses — the treble range is the same as soprano range, so it's basically S.A.T.B.

4) An <u>all-female choir</u> has <u>two groups of sopranos</u> and <u>two groups of altos</u>.

*These are the names for smaller groups:*

*2 singers = a duet*
*3 singers = a trio*
*4 singers = a quartet*
*5 singers = a quintet*
*6 singers = a sextet*

## No excuses — get on and learn all the voices...

The different voices don't just sound different in <u>pitch</u> — they've <u>got</u> different characters too, e.g. sopranos usually sound very clear and <u>glassy</u>, and basses sound more rough and <u>gravelly</u>.

*Section Seven — Instruments*

# Wind, Brass and Jazz Bands

In your listening exam, you'll get marks for saying what type of group's playing.
<u>Wind</u>, <u>jazz</u> and <u>brass</u> bands can sound quite <u>similar</u>, so make sure you know the differences.

## Wind Bands have Woodwind, Brass and Percussion

1) Wind bands are <u>largish groups</u> of instruments with 'wind' instruments — woodwind and brass — and percussion instruments.

2) There's <u>no string section</u>. If there was it would be an orchestra...

3) <u>Military bands</u> — the ones that play as they march along — are wind bands.

## Brass Bands Have Brass and Percussion

1) A brass band is a group of <u>brass</u> and <u>percussion</u> instruments.

2) A typical brass band would have <u>cornets</u>, <u>flugel horns</u>, <u>tenor</u> and <u>baritone horns</u>, <u>tenor</u> and <u>bass trombones</u>, <u>euphoniums</u>, and <u>tubas</u>.

3) The exact <u>percussion instruments</u> depend on the piece being played.

4) Brass bands have been popular in <u>England</u> for <u>years</u>.

5) <u>Contests</u> are organised through the year to find out which bands are 'best'. There's a <u>league system</u> similar to football. The divisions are called <u>sections</u>. There are <u>four sections</u> and bands are <u>promoted</u> and <u>demoted</u> each year depending on how they do at the <u>regional</u> and <u>national</u> contests.

## Jazz Bands are Quite Varied

1) Jazz bands have <u>no fixed set of instruments</u>. That's jazz... man...

2) Small jazz groups are known as <u>combos</u>. A typical combo might include a <u>trumpet</u>, <u>trombone</u>, <u>clarinet</u>, <u>saxophone</u>, <u>piano</u>, <u>banjo</u>, <u>double bass</u> and <u>drum kit</u> — but there's no fixed rule.
Combos play in small venues like <u>clubs</u> and <u>bars</u>.

3) Larger jazz bands are known as <u>big bands</u> or <u>swing bands</u>.
Instruments are doubled and tripled up so you get a <u>much bigger sound</u>.
Big bands were really popular in the <u>1930s</u> and <u>1940s</u>.
They played live at <u>dance halls</u>.

4) A large jazz band with a string section is called a <u>jazz orchestra</u>.

## Jazz Bands have a Rhythm Section and a Front Line

In a jazz band, players are either in the <u>rhythm section</u> or the <u>front line</u>.

1) The <u>rhythm section</u> is the instruments responsible for <u>keeping the beat</u> and <u>adding the harmony parts</u>. The rhythm section's usually made up of the <u>drum kit</u> with a <u>double</u> or <u>electric bass</u>, <u>electric guitar</u> and <u>piano</u>.

2) The instruments that <u>play the melody</u> are the <u>front line</u>. This is usually <u>clarinets</u>, <u>saxophones</u> and <u>trumpets</u>, but could also be guitar or violin.

## Mmmmm... jazz — everybody's favourite...

The examiners jurst lurve to set <u>multiple choice</u> questions asking what kind of band's playing, so it's best to know your stuff. In the real world outside of Music GCSE it's more important to know what a <u>jazz bore</u> is than a jazz band, so you can avoid him — he'll be all in black, probably a polo neck and smoking.

# Chamber Music

Chamber music is music composed for <u>small groups</u>. It's the kind of thing you hear at fancy weddings...

## Chamber Music was Originally 'Home Entertainment'

1) '<u>Chamber</u>' is an old word for a room in a posh building like a palace or a mansion.

2) <u>Rich people</u> could afford to <u>pay musicians</u> to come and play in their 'chambers'. Musical families could play the music for themselves. The music written for these private performances is what's called <u>chamber music</u>.

3) Nowadays, you're more likely to hear chamber music in a <u>concert hall</u> or on a <u>CD</u> than live at someone's house. Let's face it — most people haven't got the cash to hire musicians for the evening and they've now got stereos instead.

## Chamber Music is Played by Small Groups

1) The rooms where musicians came to play were nice and <u>big</u> — but <u>not enormous</u>. Limited space meant that chamber music was written for a <u>small number</u> of musicians — between <u>two</u> and <u>eight</u>.

2) There's a <u>name</u> for each size of group:

> Duet = two players
> Trio = three players
> Quartet = four players
> Quintet = five players
> Sextet = six players
> Septet = seven players
> Octet = eight players

*Have a look at the names for singing groups on P. 53 — they're much the same. Two gobbets of knowledge for the price of one...*

3) With so <u>few people</u> in chamber groups, you <u>don't</u> need a conductor. Instead, one of the players <u>leads</u>. The others have to <u>watch</u> and <u>listen</u> carefully, to make sure the <u>timing</u>, <u>dynamics</u> and <u>interpretation</u> are right.

4) Each part in the music is played by <u>just one person</u>. (That means if you stop or make a mistake everyone knows it was <u>you</u>. Scary.)

## Some Chamber Groups are Extra-Popular with Composers

Chamber music is written <u>more often</u> for some instrumental groups than others. These are some of the most <u>popular</u> types of chamber group:

| | |
|---|---|
| String trio | — violin, viola, cello |
| String quartet | — first violin, second violin, viola, cello |
| Piano trio | — piano, violin, cello (*not* three pianos) |
| Clarinet quintet | — clarinet, first violin, second violin, viola, cello (*not* five clarinets) |

## A piano trio has nothing to do with biscuits — shame...

In a way, any <u>small group</u> of musicians playing in a <u>private house</u> is chamber music. But I don't think asking a bunch of mates round to play thrash metal in the garage counts. Not strictly speaking, anyway.

*Section Seven — Instruments*

56

# The Orchestra

If you go to a classical concert, more often than not there'll be an <u>orchestra</u> up there on the stage. Loads and loads of classical music's been written for orchestra so I suppose they have to play it.

## A Modern Orchestra has Four Sections

If you go and see a <u>modern symphony orchestra</u> perform, it'll have <u>four sections</u> of instruments — strings (P.49), woodwind (P.48), brass (P.47) and percussion (P.52). The strings, woodwind, brass and percussion always sit in the <u>same places</u>.

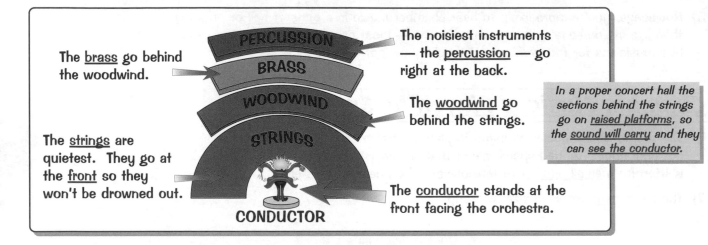

The <u>brass</u> go behind the woodwind.

The noisiest instruments — the <u>percussion</u> — go right at the back.

The <u>woodwind</u> go behind the strings.

The <u>strings</u> are quietest. They go at the <u>front</u> so they won't be drowned out.

*In a proper concert hall the sections behind the strings go on <u>raised platforms</u>, so the <u>sound will carry</u> and they can <u>see the conductor</u>.*

The <u>conductor</u> stands at the front facing the orchestra.

## The Conductor has got a Complete Overview

1) The conductor has a <u>score</u> — a version of the piece with <u>all the parts</u>. The <u>parts</u> are arranged in a <u>standard order</u>, one on top of the other so that it's easy to see what any part is doing at any time. Woodwind parts are written at the <u>top</u>, followed by brass, percussion and strings at the <u>bottom</u>.

2) The conductor <u>controls the tempo</u> by beating time with their hands, or a <u>baton</u> — a pointy white stick that's easy to see. There's a different way of beating time for each time signature.

3) The conductor <u>'cues in'</u> musicians — especially helpful for brass and percussion, who sometimes don't play anything for hundreds of bars, then suddenly have to play a really loud, important bit.

4) The conductor <u>interprets</u> the music. A conductor can decide whether to play one bit louder than another, whether to play a section in a moody or a magical way, and whether to make a piece sound very smooth or very edgy. They're a bit like a <u>film director</u> deciding the best way to <u>tell a story</u>.

The great composer and conductor Manuel Du-Pont insisted on the best possible overview of his orchestra.

## An Orchestra is Any Large Group with Strings

<u>Symphony orchestras</u> (above) are the biggest type of orchestra. There are <u>other</u> smaller kinds too:

1) <u>String orchestra</u> — an orchestra with <u>stringed instruments</u> only.
2) <u>Chamber orchestra</u> — a <u>mini-orchestra</u>. It has a small string section, a wind and brass section with <u>one or two</u> of each instrument (but <u>no</u> tubas or trombones) and a small percussion section.
3) <u>Jazz orchestra</u> — a largish jazz group with an added string section.

## Copper's a good conductor — but Barenboim's better...

Copy out the diagram of the orchestra (without words) then close the book and fill in the different instrument sections in the right places. Then learn all the bumph about the conductor and the different orchestras.

*Section Seven — Instruments*

# Music Technology

Modern technological and 'virtual' instruments mean that you can muck about with a lot more sounds nowadays than you could in *ye olden times*. Moby eat your heart out...

## MIDI lets you Connect Electronic Musical Instruments

1) MIDI was invented in 1983. It stands for Musical Instrument Digital Interface. It's a way of connecting different electronic instruments.
2) MIDI equipment is connected by MIDI cables.
3) MIDI data is digital information (i.e. in zeroes and ones). It's sent down the MIDI cables. MIDI instruments turn MIDI information into sound (or vice versa).
4) One important advantage of MIDI is that it's allowed musical equipment to be linked with computers, opening up a complete new world of music-making.

## Synthesizers let you Make New Sounds

Synthesizers come in different forms, like keyboard synthesizers and synthesizer modules (without keyboards). The point of them is to let you create new sounds. There are different types of synthesizers:

1) Analogue synthesizers were mainly made in the 70s and early 80s. They've often got lots of knobs and sliders — you use these to change the sound.
2) Digital synthesizers started to be popular in the 80s. Almost all modern synthesizers are digital. They usually have less knobs and sliders than analogue synths.
3) Software synths started to become popular in the late 90s. Software synths are computer programs (often linked to a sequencer). They often have graphical sliders and knobs that you can move with a mouse. Some of them emulate analogue and early digital synthesizers.

## Samplers let you 'Pinch' other people's Sounds

1) A sampler is a piece of equipment that can record, process (change) and play back sections of pre-recorded sound — samples.
2) Samplers are often used to take a bit of a piece of music that's already been recorded and use that in some new music.

> REMIX *is a term used for a different version of a piece of music. Remixes are often made of pop and rock tunes to turn them into dance music (they're often speeded up and given a fast dance drum beat).*

## Sequencers let you Record, Edit and Replay Music

1) Sequencer is the posh word for equipment that can record (save), edit (mess about with) and replay music stored as MIDI information. Modern sequencers are usually computer programs.
2) Many lines (tracks) of music can be played back at the same time.
3) Each track can be given its own set of instructions, e.g. instrument or volume levels.
4) One of the big advantages of a sequencer is that it shows your music as actual notation or as representative boxes — this makes it much easier to change and try out new ideas.
5) Nowadays, most sequencers can record audio (real sounds) as well as the MIDI stuff so you can create MIDI music and then record your own voice or instruments along with it. Lots of music is recorded using sequencers now.
6) Modern sequencing programs often include synthesizers and samplers as well.
7) Drum machines are special sequencers that play back rhythm patterns using built-in drum sounds.

## And now the end is near...

Even if you don't use music technology, other people do — that means you need to know how it's used to create certain styles of music. Learn the basic function of each type of equipment. One lot of revision summary questions, and a handy little glossary to go — and you're done.

# Revision Summary

*Trrr-rrr-rrr. Trrr-rrr-rrr.* [Drum roll] *Pa-pa-pa-pa-pa-pa. Paa-paa-paa-paa-paa-paa.* [Trumpets] Ladies and gentlemen, the final Revision Summary of the final section is about to commence. Take your seats in the auditorium, sit back, and marvel at the wonders of the last page not including the Glossary and Index.

1) What are brass instruments made of?

2) Name three brass instruments.

3) How do you vary the pitch on a brass instrument?

4) Are all woodwind instruments made of wood?

5) Name three woodwind instruments.

6) What are the three different mouthpieces used on woodwind instruments called?
   How do they work?

7) What are all those little keys, springs and levers for on a woodwind instrument?

8) What's the smallest string instrument?

9) What's the biggest one that you play with a bow?

10) What makes a harp different from the other string instruments? Give three differences.

11) Where would you put a mute on a bowed string instrument and what effect would it have?

12) How do you make different notes on a string instrument?

13) How many strings are there on:
    a) an acoustic guitar     b) an electric guitar     c) a bass guitar

14) What do you call those metal bits on the fingerboard of a guitar? Do you get them on a bass?

15) What's the proper word for twanging a guitar string with a plectrum?

16) Name three different keyboard instruments.

17) What's the biggest type of keyboard instrument?

18) What's the most popular keyboard instrument?

19) How could you tell you were listening to a church organ and not a harpsichord?

20) Name three tuned percussion instruments and six untuned percussion instruments.

21) What's the highest type of singing voice?

22) What's the lowest type of singing voice?

23) What do you call a boy's voice when it's got the same range as a soprano?

24) How can you tell the difference between a wind band and a brass band?

25) How can you tell the difference between a wind band and a jazz orchestra?

26) What are the two sections of a jazz orchestra called, and what are their jobs?

27) Why's chamber music called chamber music?

28) How many people are there in:  a) a trio     b) a sextet     c) a quartet     d) an octet?

29) How many clarinets are there in a clarinet quintet?

30) Sketch a plan of a standard symphony orchestra. Label the different sections and the conductor.

31) What sections are there in a string orchestra, chamber orchestra and jazz orchestra?

32) What does MIDI stand for?

33) How is MIDI information stored?

34) Write a definition of:  a) a synthesizer     b) a sampler     c) a sequencer.

# Glossary & Index

There are millions of symbols and tricky words that get bandied about in music. Look up any that fox you here — I've done my darndest to squeeze 'em all in. Follow the page reference to find out more.

## A

**accent** > Goes over a note and means "give it more bite".

*a tempo* Go back to the original tempo. **10**

**abrupt modulation** Sudden **modulation** in the middle of a piece, often to the **key** one **semitone** above. **30**

*accelerando* or *accel.* Speed up the **tempo**. **10**

**accidental** **Sharp**, **flat** or **natural** symbol used when a note's needed that's not part of the **home key**. **5**

*adagio* Play at 66-76 beats per minute. Slightly faster than **largo**. **10**

*agitato* Play in an agitated way. **10**

*alla marcia* Play in a march style. **10**

*allargando* or *allarg.* Slow down the tempo and play more broadly (and a little louder). **10**

*allegro* 120-168 beats per minute. Lively. **10**

**alto voice** Voice that sings roughly in the range from the F below middle C to the F at the top of the treble clef stave. **4, 53**

*amoroso* Play in a romantic, loving way. **10**

*andante* 76-108 beats a minute. Walking pace. **10**

**anthem** Short **polyphonic** choir piece performed in Protestant churches. **41**

**aria** Song for a soloist in an **opera**. **40**

**arpeggio** The notes of a **chord** played in succession, either going up or down. **26**

*assai* very, e.g. *assai presto* means 'very fast'

**augmentation** Multiplying the length of notes in a tune to get a new version of it. **35, 45**

**augmented interval** An interval that's a **semitone** larger than a **major** or **perfect** interval. **19**

**augmented triad** **Triad** that's got four **semitones** (a **major third**) between the bottom note and middle note and four semitones between the middle and top notes. **22**

**auxiliary note** An **ornamental note**. **12**

## B

**baroque** Musical style of the seventeenth and early eighteenth centuries. Strong bass and lots of **ornamentation**. **44**

**bass voice** Voice that sings roughly in the range from F below the bass clef to the E just above middle C. **53**

**baton** Pointy white stick used by **conductors** to show the beat. **56**

**binary form** Form of music in two distinct sections. **34**

**block chord** Chord played by sounding all notes at once. **26**

**brass band** Band with brass and percussion sections. **54**

**breathing mark** ' Symbol telling brass and wind players to take a breath.

**bridge** Section in a piece of music used to link two different chunks together. **37, 38**

**broken chord** Chord that's played as a series of notes. **26**

## C

**cadence** Pair of chords used to finish off a phrase. **28**

*calmato* Play the music so it sounds very calm. **10**

**cantata** Like an **oratorio**, but using words from books or the Bible. **41**

**chamber music** Music for small groups, originally written to be performed in people's houses. **55**

**chamber orchestra** Orchestra with small string and percussion sections, and one or two of each wind and brass instrument. No tubas, no trombones — too loud. **56**

**chorale** Hymn for a choir. **41**

**chord progression** Repeated pattern of related chords used in bass and rhythm parts, especially **ground bass**. **26**

**chord symbols** *C, C+, Cm maj7* Symbols like these are shorthand for different chords. **22**

**chromatic scale** 13-note scale containing <u>all</u> the notes (tones and semitones) within an **octave**. **17**

**chromatic decoration** **Ornamental notes** not in **home key**. **27**

**circle of fifths** Madly complicated diagram showing how all the keys relate to each other. **16**

**clarinet quintet** Small group with clarinet, 2 violins, viola and cello. **55**

**classical** <u>Either</u> any music that's not pop (or jazz, folk, hip-hop, R&B etc.), <u>or</u> music composed in Europe in the late 18th and early 19th centuries. **51**

**coda** Bit at the end of a song that's different from the rest, and finishes it off nicely. **37, 38**

*col legno* For string players — play the string with the back of the bow instead of bowing. **49**

**compound time** Time signature where each main beat can be split into three little ones. **7**

*con sordino* Play with a **mute**. **49**

**concerto** Piece for an orchestra with a soloist, in three movements. **39**

**concord** Nice sound that you get when notes are played together. **21**

**conductor** Bossy individual, who stands at the front of the orchestra waving hands or a white stick to make sure they stick to the beat and know what's going on. **56**

**contrapuntal** = **polyphonic** **31**

**countermelody** Extra tune played at the same time as the theme to make sure things don't get boring. **35**

**crescendo** ◁ Get louder gradually. **11**

## D

*da capo* or *D.C.* Start again from the beginning.

*da capo al fine* Go back to the beginning and play all the way through till you get to the sign that says *fine*.

*dal segno* or *D.S.* Start again from the sign — 𝄋.

**decorative note** = **ornamental note**. **12, 27**

**descant** Higher tune sung or played at the same time as the main tune and harmonising with it. **31**

**diatonic decoration** **Ornamental notes** in **home key**. **12, 27**

**diminished interval** Interval that's one **semitone** smaller than a minor or **perfect** interval. **19**

**diminished triad** **Triad** that's got three **semitones** (a **minor third**) between the bottom note and middle note and three semitones between the middle and top notes. **22**

**diminuendo** ▷ Get quieter gradually. **11**

**diminution** Dividing the length of notes in a tune to get a new version of it. The opposite of **augmentation**. **35, 45**

**discord** or **dissonance** Horrible sound that you get when notes that don't go are played together. **21**

# Glossary & Index

# Glossary & Index

**minor triad** **Triad** with an **interval** of three **semitones** between the bottom note and middle note (a **minor third**), and four **semitones** between the middle and top notes (a **major third**). **22**

**minuet** Third movement of a **sonata** or **symphony**. Style developed from a seventeenth century dance, so it's quite lively. Third movement can also be a **scherzo**. **39**

*moderato* 108-120 beats per minute. Not too fast, not too slow. Moderate speed. **10**

**modes** Eight note scales following particular sequences of tones and semitones. **17**

**modulation** When music shifts from the **home key** into another key, usually a related one. **30**

*molto* Italian for "very". You often see it before other instructions, e.g. *"molto allegro"* means "very lively"

**monophonic** Music with a tune and nothing else. No backing, rhythm or harmony. Just you and your kazoo. **31**

**motet** Short **polyphonic** choir piece performed in Catholic churches. **41**

**mordents** ∿ and ∿ Twiddly **ornaments**. **12**

**mute** Wooden, rubber or metal gadget used to dampen the sound of brass and string instruments. **47, 49**

## N

**natural** ♮ Symbol shows you shouldn't **sharpen** or **flatten** the note. **5**

**natural minor scale** 8-note **minor scale** using the notes of the **minor key** (and no funny accidentals like the **melodic** and **harmonic minors**). **15**

**Note** ♩ Different symbols stand for different lengths of note. For all the main ones see page **8**.

## O

**octave** The distance from one note to the next note up or down with the same letter name. **14**

**octet** Piece in eight parts or group of eight players. **55**

**offbeat** Offbeat music puts the main accent anywhere except the first beat of the bar (the usual place for it). **45**

**opera** Massive compositions telling massive stories using massive tunes, massive singers and massive budgets. **40**

**oratorio** Like an opera, but with a religious story, and not acted out. **40**

**ornamental notes** Tiny, short notes added as frills to the tune. **12**

**ostinato** A musical pattern (e.g. a bass part) which repeats over and over again. The tune varies around it. **44**

## P

**passing note** Linking note. **27**

**pause** ⌒ Sign placed over a note, chord or rest to indicate that the normal time value is prolonged. **10**

**pentatonic scales** 5-note scale used in folk music. A major pentatonic uses notes 1, 2, 3, 5 and 6 of an ordinary **major scale**. A minor pentatonic uses notes 1, 3, 4, 5 and 7 of a **natural minor scale**. **17**

**perfect interval** There are three perfect intervals: between the first note of a scale and the fourth note; the first note and the fifth; and the **octave**. **19**

**perfect cadence** **Cadence** going from chord V to I. **29**

*pesante* Play in a heavy, peasanty style. Imagine your wellies are full of mud and you've had too much cider. **10**

**phrase** A few bars or notes that hang together to make a group. **28**

*pianissimo* **pp** Very quiet. **11**

*piano* **p** Quiet. **11**

**piano trio** One piano, one violin and one cello. **55**

**pitch** How high or low a note is. **3, 8**

*più* "More". You could see it in phrases like *"più agitato"* — "more agitated".

**pivot chord** Chord that belongs to two **keys**. It's used to shift a piece of music from one key to another (**modulate**) because it sounds OK in both. **30**

**plagal cadence** **Cadence** going from chord I V to I. **29**

*poco* "A little bit". You could see it in phrases like *"un poco più agitato"* — "a bit more agitated".

**polyphonic** Music with two or more tunes played at the same time and woven together. **31**

*presto* 180-200 beats per minute. Really fast. About as fast as it gets. **10**

**primary chords** **Root note** chord, and chords IV and V. These are the easiest ones to harmonise with. **23**

## Q

**quartet** Piece in four parts, or a group with four players. **31, 53, 55**

**quintet** Piece in five parts, or a group with five players. **53, 55**

## R

*rallentando, rall.* = *ritenuto*. **10**

**recitative** Bits in **opera** when the characters talk over a simple accompaniment from the orchestra. **40**

**repeat** 𝄆 𝄇 Play everything between the signs twice. If you see this — 𝄢 — play the notes in the first bar first time round and the notes in the second bar next time round. **34**

**rhythm section** Instruments that keep the rhythm in a jazz band, e.g. double bass, drum kit, bass guitar, piano. **54**

**rhythmic chords** Chords played in a rhythmic way so you get rhythm and **harmony**. **26**

**riff** Repeated **phrase** played over and over again. Mostly used in pop, rock and jazz. **36**

*risoluto* Play in a confident, decided way. **10**

*ritenuto, rit.* Gradually slow down. Means much the same as *rallentando*. **10**

**rondo** A way of structuring music so you start with one tune, go on to a new one, go back to the first one, on to another new one, back to the first one, on to a new one... as many times as you like. **34**

**root chord** Chord with its **root note** at the bottom. **24**

**root note** The note a chord originates from, e.g. in a C major chord, the root note would be C. **21**

*rubato, rub.* You don't have to stick too closely to the **tempo**. **10**

## S

**S.A.T.B.** Short for "sopranos, altos, tenors and basses", the four sections in a standard choir. **53**

# Glossary & Index

**scale** A set pattern of notes all from the same **key**. The most common ones in Western music are **major** and **minor** scales. **14, 15**

**scherzo** Lively third movement of a symphony or sonata. Wakes the audience up in time for the final movement. **39**

**score** **Conductor**'s version of a piece of orchestral music, with all the parts in. **56**

**semitone** The gap in **pitch** between e.g. A and A♯, E♭ and E or B and C. On a piano keyboard, any two notes, black or white, immediately next to each other are a semitone apart. **3**

*senza sordino* Take off the **mute** (after *con sordino*).

**septet** Piece in seven parts or group with seven players. **55**

**sequencing** Repeating **phrases** but changing the **pitch**. The **intervals** between notes stay the same. **44**

**sextet** Piece in six parts or group with six players. **53, 55**

*sforzando* **sf** Play very loud, very suddenly on the note that the little symbol sits over.

*simile, sim.* "Do the same thing again."

**sharp** ♯ Symbol shows you should play the note a semitone higher. **5**

**simple time** Time signature with two, three or four basic beats. **7**

**slash chord** Chord symbol used to show an **inversion**, e.g. "D/F♯" means "play a D major chord, with F♯ at the bottom". **24**

**slur** Curved line joining notes of different **pitch**. Means you should go smoothly from one to the next. **11**

**sonata** Piece of music in three or four movements for a soloist or duet. First movement is always in **sonata form**. **39**

**sonata form** Piece of music with two main **themes**. These are introduced in the first bit, developed in the middle bit and repeated in the last bit. **38**

**soprano voice** Voice that sings roughly in the range from middle C to two octaves above that. Some singers can go even higher — eeek. **4, 53**

*sospirando* Play in a sighing sort of a way. **10**

**staccato** Play each note slightly short and very separate from the ones either side. **11**

**string orchestra** Orchestra with violins, violas, cellos and double basses only. **56**

**string quartet** Two violins, a viola and a cello. **55**

**string trio** A violin, a viola and a cello. **55**

**subdominant** Fourth note in a major or minor scale. **14, 23**

**submediant** Sixth note in a major or minor scale. **14, 23**

**supertonic** Second note in a major or minor scale. **14, 23**

**suspension** A three note series that momentarily clashes with the accompanying chords. **27**

**symphony** Long meaty piece of music, in three or four movements, for a full orchestra. **39**

**symphony orchestra** An orchestra with just about every acoustic instrument known to science (except for keyboards). Sometimes there's a choir too. **56**

**syncopated** The accents are shifted from the main beat to a weaker beat, to avoid a regular rhythm. E.g. in $\frac{4}{4}$ time the main accent would usually fall on the first beat — whereas in syncopated $\frac{4}{4}$ time you could move the accent to, say, the second beat. **45**

## T

**tempo** Speed. **10**

**tenor voice** Voice that sings roughly in the range from the C below middle C to the G above. **53**

*tenuto* Hold each note for as long as possible.

**ternary form** Piece in three sections. The first and last are much the same. The middle one's a bit different and in a different (but related) key. **34, 43**

**theme** Musical idea. The bit you hum. **35**

**tie** Curved line that joins two notes of the same pitch, so when they're played they sound like one note. **9**

**time signature** Numbers at the beginning of a piece that tell you how many beats in a bar. **2, 6**

**tone** The gap in **pitch** between e.g. A and B, E♭ and F or G and A. One tone = two **semitones**. **3**

**tonic** First note in a major or minor scale. **14, 23**

**treble** Pre-pubescent boy who sings like a girl... I mean a **soprano**. **53**

*tremolo* Play in a trembly, nervous sounding way. **49**

**triad** 3-note chord which uses a **root**, a third above and a fifth above. **21**

**trill** *tr* Twiddly **ornament**. **12**

**tritone** Uncomfortable-sounding interval of three tones. **19**

*troppo* Too much. You're more likely to see "*ma non troppo*", "but not too much".

**trio** Piece with three parts, or group with three players. **31, 53, 55**

*trionfale* Play in a triumphant, confident-sounding way. **10**

**turns** ∽ ∾ etc. Twiddly **ornaments**. **12**

*tutti* Everyone plays together. **31**

**twelve-bar blues** Style of blues with a 12-bar repeating chord pattern. **36**

## U

**unison** Everyone plays or sings the same notes. **31**

**up bow** V Symbol for string players telling them to bow from the tip of the bow.

## V

**variation form** Variation form has lots of smallish sections. The first one is the main theme, and the rest are variations on the theme. **35** (**variations** also on **p. 38**)

*vivace* Play fast and lively. **10**

## W

**Western Art Music** = Western Classical music

**whole tone scale** 7-note scale with a tone between each note and the next. **17**

**wind band** Band with woodwind, brass and percussion sections. **54**